Everyman's Poetry

Everyman, I will go with thee,
and be thy guide

Michelangelo

Translated and edited by CHRISTOPHER RYAN

University of Sussex

EVERYMAN

J. M. Dent · London

Introduction and other critical apparatus
© J. M. Dent 1998

J. M. Dent
Orion Publishing Group
Orion House
5 Upper St Martin's Lane
London WC2H 9EA

Typeset by Deltatype Ltd, Birkenhead, Merseyside
Printed in Great Britain by
The Guernsey Press Co. Ltd, Guernsey, C.I.

British Library Cataloguing-in-Publication
Data is available on request

ISBN 0 460 87963 4

Contents

Note on the Author and Editor/Translator

MICHELANGELO (1475–1564) can lay claim to the title of best known and most appreciated artist of the Italian Renaissance: he is universally recognized as being, within the field of the visual arts, a many-sided genius, with masterpieces of outstanding originality in sculpture, painting, drawing and architecture. What is less well known is that his creativity extended to the field of literature: he was the first artist in the Western tradition to leave a substantial body of poetry (amounting to 302 pieces in the latest critical edition). In addition to producing such visual masterpieces as his statue of *David* in Florence, and his paintings of the *Creation* and the *Last Judgement* in the Sistine Chapel in Rome, Michelangelo devoted himself with flair, subtlety and vigour to finding words to express the emotions and interests that gripped his soul. His poems explore in a highly distinctive style the great themes of love, beauty, the transience of life and the yearning for acceptance and salvation. Long valued by a small circle of *cognoscenti*, his poetry is beginning to establish itself as one of the major achievements of Italian Renaissance literature. Dense, vivid and idiosyncratic, it throws a unique light both on the personality of the great visual artist and on the principal poetic, intellectual and religious concerns of one of the most vibrant periods in Western culture.

CHRISTOPHER RYAN studied at the Gregorian University, Rome, and the Universities of Glasgow and Cambridge. He has taught at several universities in North America and England, and is now Professor of Italian at the University of Sussex. He has just published a major study, *The Poetry of Michelangelo: An Introduction* (London: Athlone Press, 1998).

Chronology of Michelangelo's Life

Year	Age	Life
1475–96		
		Michelangelo is born on 6 March at Caprese, near Arezzo, while his father holds a temporary political post there; the family home is in Florence
1481	6	Death of his mother
1487	12	Apprenticed in the painting studio of the brothers Ghirlandaio
1489	14	Begins training in sculpture in the Medici garden museum, under the patronage of Lorenzo the Magnificent
1492	17	Continues in the Casa de' Medici under Lorenzo's son Piero
		Among major works of this period are the *Battle of the Centaurs* and the *Madonna of the Steps*
1496–1501		
1496	21	Begins first period in Rome
		His main works of this first Roman period are the *Bacchus* and the St Peter's *Pietà*

Chronology of his Times

Year	Artistic Events	Historical Context
1481	Landino's edition of Dante's *Commedia*	
1483	Birth of Raphael	
1485	Birth of Titian	
1492	Death of Lorenzo de' Medici	Columbus's voyage to America Election of Pope Alexander VI
1494	Death of Poliziano	French invasion of Naples Expulsion of the Medici from Florence
1498		Execution of Savonarola
1499	Death of Ficino	Fall of Milan to the French

Year	Age	Life
1501–5		
1501	26	Returns to Florence; begins work on the *David*
1503	28	Begins writing poetry about this time
1504	29	Completes the *David*, which was erected in front of the Palazzo della Signoria
		His other major works of his second Florentine period include the *Doni Madonna*, the *Taddei Tondo*, the *Pitti Tondo*, the *Bruges Madonna* and the cartoon for *The Battle of Cascina* (now lost)
1505–17		
1505	30	Begins his second period spent mainly in Rome, having been summoned there by Pope Julius II to build his tomb
1506	31	Difficulties over the Julius tomb lead to a two-year absence from Rome, in Florence (1506), in Bologna (1506–8) and Florence again (1508)
1508	33	Begins work on the ceiling of the Sistine Chapel
1512	37	Completes the ceiling of the Sistine Chapel
1513	38	Begins work on the Julius tomb
		His major works of his second Roman period, in addition to the painting of the Sistine Ceiling, include the bronze statue of Julius II (done in Bologna, destroyed in 1512), two *Slaves* or *Prisoners* (now in the Louvre) and the *Moses*
1517–34		
1517	42	Begins his third period spent mainly in Florence, having returned there at the request of Pope Leo X, to work on the façade of the church of San Lorenzo (a project never realized)

Year	Artistic Events	Historical Context
1503		Election of Pope Julius II Spanish victory over French at Garigliano
1506		Laying of the foundation stone of the new St Peter's, Rome
1510	Death of Botticelli Death of Giorgione	
1512		Restoration of the Medici in Florence
1513	Machiavelli, *The Prince*	Election of Pope Leo X (Giovanni de' Medici)
1516	Castiglione, *Il libro del cortegiano* Ariosto, *Orlando furioso*	
1517		Luther presents his ninety-five theses at Wittenburg

Year	Age	Life
1519	44	Begins work on the Medici Chapel (= the New Sacristy) in San Lorenzo, while continuing work on the Julius tomb
1524	49	Begins work on the Laurentian Library
1527	52	Helps fortify Florence on behalf of the short-lived republic, during the years 1527–30
1528	53	Death of his favourite brother, Buonarroto
1532	57	Meets Tommaso Cavalieri during a visit to Rome; beginning of his greatest period of poetic creativity His major artistic works of his third Florentine period include four *Slaves* or *Prisoners* (now in the Accademia in Florence), the *Victory*, *Leda and the Swan* (now lost), several presentation drawings, and, above all, the Medici chapel with its tombs and figures and the Laurentian Library

1534–64

Year	Age	Life
1534	59	Begins his third period in Rome, where he lives until his death; commissioned by the new pope, Paul III, to continue with the plan of Pope Clement VII to fresco the east wall of the Sistine Chapel
1536	61	Starts work on the *Last Judgement* fresco; meets Vittoria Colonna

Year	Artistic Events	Historical Context
1518	Birth of Tintoretto	
1519	Death of Leonardo	Election of Emperor Charles V
		Magellan's voyage
1520	Death of Raphael	
1521		French defeated at Ravenna
		Luther excommunicated
		Death of Pope Leo X
1523		Election of Pope Clement VII
		(Giulio de' Medici)
1525	Bembo, *Prose della volgar lingua*	French defeated at Pavia
		Beginning of Spanish hegemony in Italy
1527		Sack of Rome
		Fall of the Medici in Florence
1528	Birth of Veronese	
1529		Crowning of Charles V at Bologna
1530		Restoration of the Medici in Florence
1534	Rabelais, *Gargantua*	England secedes from Roman jurisdiction
		Election of Pope Paul III
		Cosimo de' Medici becomes Duke of Florence

Year	Age	Life
1541	66	Completes the *Last Judgement*
1542	67	Begins the frescos of the Pauline Chapel
1546	71	Death of Luigi del Riccio
1547	72	Death of Vittoria Colonna; death of Sebastiano del Piombo; end of his great period of poetic creativity; unveiling of the much-reduced Julius tomb in the church of S. Pietro ad Vincola, Rome
1555	80	Death of his brother Sigismondo, and of his loyal assistant and servant Urbino
1563	88	Elected an academician of the Florentine *Accademia del Disegno*
1564	88	Dies 18 February
		His other major works of this third Roman period include the *Brutus*, and the Florence *Pietà* and Rondanini *Pietà* of his final years; after 1549 he worked principally as an architect, his two main projects being the planning and redesigning of the Capitol and of St Peter's, the twin symbolic centres of secular and sacred Rome

Year	Artistic Events	Historical Context
1541		Diet of Ratisbon
1545		Opening of the Council of Trent
1550	Vasari, *Lives of the Artists*	Election of Pope Julius III
1555		Election of Pope Paul IV
		Treaty of Augsburg
1556		Abdication of Charles V
1559		Treaty of Câteau-Cambrésis
1563		Closure of the Council of Trent
1564	Birth of Galileo	

Introduction

Michelangelo was the first major artist in the Western tradition to leave a significant body of poetry (302 pieces in the standard modern edition). Any reader not aware of this is in good company: many, perhaps even most, of those who pride themselves on being able instantly to identify any of Michelangelo's major works of art know nothing of his considerable poetic achievement.

Indeed the fault – if fault there be – is not all on the readers' part. It was only comparatively recently that a comprehensive critical edition of Michelangelo's poetry was published (by E. N. Girardi, in 1960), setting it out in broad chronological order. Moreover, the poetry often does not make easy reading: the style is almost always dense, and frequently rough (with even occasional faulty grammar). It is, none the less, well on its way now to establishing itself as a major poetic achievement of the Renaissance period and of Western poetry generally. What lies behind the recent resurgence in interest, and justifies the effort required to become familiar with this difficult but rewarding poetry? Three reasons may be suggested.

It seems merely a matter of commonsense to acknowledge that most of us come to Michelangelo's poetry in order to understand and appreciate better the outstanding artist. Light is thrown, and with intensity, on the artist himself, in a whole variety of ways. Not infrequently we will, through the poetry, touch the source of the great impulses that animated Michelangelo in his artistic enterprises: his inspiration by beauty, principally human beauty; his aspiring through that finite beauty towards an infinite beauty and goodness which he saw as powerfully and exquisitely, but only very partially, reflected in this world; his sense of life as a constant struggle against the ever threatening ravages of physical death and moral failure. Perhaps surprisingly, if we identify Michelangelo totally with the towering genius who created monumental works in sculpture, painting and architecture, we shall encounter a highly vulnerable personality: dependent for inspiration on, for example, Tommaso Cavalieri, a young man of outstanding physical and personal beauty by whom Michelangelo was captivated when he met him in 1532, as his own sixth decade was drawing to a close. Perhaps more surprisingly still, in the man notorious for his *terribilità*, we shall discover a comic element, displayed not least in a vein of self-mockery that gleams throughout his poetic life, from his parodying of the awkward position he had to adopt to paint the Sistine Ceiling (poem 2 here) to the unflinching irony of his description of the ailments that afflicted him in old age (poem 92). The poetry is, in short, an invaluable way of coming to know the personality of Michelangelo, whose very stature as an artist has tended to obscure the complexity of his character.

Whatever our original motivation in coming to Michelangelo's poetry, that poetry is also rewarding simply as poetry, and brings its own very particular poetic pleasure. Sometimes, indeed quite frequently, Michelangelo's poetic artistry is readily appreciable, as in the opening lines of one of the most famous sonnets of his last years (poem 98):

> Giunto è già 'l corso della vita mia
> con tempestoso mar, per fragil barca,
> al comun porto, ov'a render si varca
> conto e ragion d'ogni opra trista e pia.

(My life's journey has finally arrived, after a stormy sea, in a fragile boat, at the common port, through which all must pass to render an account and explanation of their every act, evil and devout.)

Here it takes very little attention to sense the firm, steady beat in the single movement of the opening line conveying the finality of arrival, and to feel the contrast with the broken rhythms of the next three half-line units which speak of the perilousness of the journey; these rhythms in turn give way in the following line-and-a-half to the smoother description of the scene that will unfold once port has been reached.

Equally if not more often, though, appreciation of the poetic qualities of Michelangelo's work does not flow readily from the page. Here familiarity with his visual art can make us sensitive to the nature of his poetic achievement. Michelangelo regarded himself first and foremost as a sculptor, and few would wish to quarrel with that self-assessment: his painting and drawing often have a quality that can best be described as sculptural. The same holds true of his poetry. This derives from several features, not least from ellipsis and inverted word order. The cumulative effect of features such as these last two is that of density and volume: the words of Michelangelo's poetry often do not so much carry us along in their flow as stand firmly before us, waiting for our eyes to focus more sharply so that the figure or figures may emerge gradually from the solid block. Or perhaps better, the apparently rough-hewn poetic object before us proves under closer scrutiny to be, certainly, unpolished, but not on that account unthoughtful, unsubtle, the work of a careless or incapable hand.

What holds true of specific lines and details applies also to many poems in their entirety: they pulse with dense energy. Here again an analogy with Michelangelo's visual art may be illuminating. It has often been observed that many of the human figures in Michelangelo's sculpture, painting and drawing catch our eye because they manifest an extreme tension: between the apparently boundless energy and aspiration that animate the figures, and the physical limits of the human form. Our admiration is frequently aroused by Michelangelo's ability to convey an infinity of spirit, as it were, energizing a finite human form without destroying or unacceptably distorting it: many of his figures are at once immensely powerful and believable. A comparable impression is created by many of his poems. There, too, he strains at the limits without finally breaking them.

There is a third way, inextricably linked to the first two, in which Michelangelo's poetry rewards the effort spent on it: put simply, it makes one think. One 'thing' that Michelangelo would not have us forget, though most of us willingly do, is the brevity of life. From his earliest to his latest poetry Michelangelo recurrently brings before his and our mind the perspective of eternity and the fact that all human life is in that perspective short; as he puts it in one simple juxtaposition: 'Chiunche nasce a morte arriva' ('Whoever is born arrives at death', poem 6). Michelangelo is not though, in his poetry as a whole (as he is not in his art as a whole), a jaundiced Jeremiah. The fleetingness of life strikes him forcibly because he so keenly appreciated life's beauties, above all human beauty, physical and personal. It is no accident that the poetic floodgates were opened for Michelangelo, transforming what was scarcely more than an occasional poetic impulse in his earlier years into a constant creative concern in his maturity, when he was captivated by the outstanding gifts of the young Cavalieri. The surge of poetry was intended to put into words an enthralment with one who by all accounts combined to an outstanding degree beauty of body and soul.

Michelangelo's poetry also stimulates us to think by bringing home to us the intensity with which he shared some of the basic tenets of his time, a period very different from our own but intellectually among the most vigorous in the evolution of Western culture. Again the poetry does this in a whole variety of ways, but one may be singled out as being perhaps as central to Michelangelo's time as it is alien to our own. Here poem 68 may be our guide. In that poem Michelangelo speaks with lucidity on what it is that inspires him in his artistic endeavours. The opening lines (1–4), where he intimates the strength of feeling with which he regarded himself as called to give expression to beauty in his art, are certainly interesting, but they are not surprising. As this short poem evolves, however, and Michelangelo elaborates on what beauty signifies for him, we enter a stranger world. Beauty alone carries the eye from this world 'to those heights' ('a quella altezza') which he sets himself to paint and sculpt (lines 5–6); the poet goes on to make it clear that the phrase referring to heights is no lightly tossed-off metaphor. He criticizes those who would drag down beauty and make it a thing of the senses (7–8), and contrasts this low view of beauty with what he simply states as being the truth (9–12), that 'la beltà ... muove / e porta al cielo ogni intelletto sano' ('beauty ... moves and carries every healthy mind to heaven'), it inspires a movement 'dal mortale al divin' ('from the mortal to the divine sphere'). As this poem briefly indicates, for Michelangelo (at least until his last years) art, and more generally the appreciation of beauty, was a religious task; by this he did not mean exclusively, nor even primarily, a church-related exercise, but a whole way of thinking about and looking at life, which affected the very texture of daily existence. For he adhered passionately to the fundamentals of Neoplatonic philosophy, such as the belief that this passing world is but the creation and reflection of a higher, immortal world, and that on this earth the supreme means of coming in contact with that divine world is beauty. The 'place' where the conjunction of physical and spiritual beauty is most evident is the human face, and particularly the eyes, which, in a person whose character matches the beauty of his (or her) face, have depths that are ultimately divine in the strictest sense. We can hope to understand Michelangelo (and one important strand in the culture of his period) with anything approaching adequacy only if we remember that for him the artistic enterprise was an endeavour to make heaven more present on earth.

Readers approaching Michelangelo's poetry for the first time may find it helpful to have some of its broad 'physical' contours mapped out. The poetry is for the most part a product of Michelangelo's late maturity and old age. The artist began writing poetry at a fairly early age, around 1503–4, but in the following thirty years wrote only about fifty poems. The turning point, as already noted, was Michelangelo's meeting with Tommaso Cavalieri, in late 1532: over the following fifteen years some 200 poems came from his pen. With the death of several close friends in 1546–7, and the increasing toll taken by illness and old age on his own body, his output understandably dropped to its original trickle (some thirty poems in his last seventeen years), although several of his final poems are among his finest. As regards genre, most of Michelangelo's poems are in three short forms: the sonnet, the madrigal and the quatrain.

A word should be said on the present translation. A number of English translations of Michelangelo's poetry exist, all in the form of poetry. It seems to me that there is a role for the modest enterprise of attempting to render Michelangelo's poetry in modern prose. Although this cannot hope to convey, as poetic translation does at its best, the strictly poetic rhythms and force of the original, it may hope to avoid the expansion or contraction of the plain sense of the original to meet different poetic demands, and, perhaps more importantly, it may hope to avoid the danger of projecting onto the original a poetic voice which will inevitably be different and to an extent alien. The need for a translation that aims above all to be clear and simply faithful may be felt particularly in cases such as that of Michelangelo, where the poetry is frequently dense and tortuous to the extent that even its basic meaning can be difficult to penetrate.

There are two sets of notes. Immediately after the translation of each poem there is a basic annotation (in parenthesis) stating genre, dedicatee where known or reasonably conjectured, and dating; such notes marked with a double dagger (‡) denote those poems which Michelangelo had intended to include in a publication which never came to fruition. At the end of the entire selection are fuller notes on many of the poems, indicated by asterisks in the translations; line numbers in these notes refer to the Italian original.

CHRISTOPHER RYAN

Note on the Text

The poems in this book are taken from Christopher Ryan's complete edition and translation, *Michelangelo: The Poems* (London: J. M. Dent 1996; paperback, 1997).

Michelangelo

1

Quanto si gode, lieta e ben contesta
di fior sopra' crin d'or d'una, grillanda,
che l'altro inanzi l'uno all'altro manda,
come ch'il primo sia a baciar la testa!
Contenta è tutto il giorno quella vesta   5
che serra 'l petto e poi par che si spanda,
e quel c'oro filato si domanda
le guanci' e 'l collo di toccar non resta.
Ma più lieto quel nastro par che goda,
dorato in punta, con sì fatte tempre   10
che preme e tocca il petto ch'egli allaccia.
E la schietta cintura che s'annoda
mi par dir seco: qui vo' stringer sempre.
Or che farebbon dunche le mie braccia?

2

I' ho già fatto un gozzo in questo stento,
come fa l'acqua a' gatti in Lombardia
o ver d'altro paese che si sia,
c'a forza 'l ventre appicca sotto 'l mento.
La barba al cielo, e la memoria sento   5
in sullo scrigno, e 'l petto fo d'arpia,
e 'l pennel sopra 'l viso tuttavia
mel fa, gocciando, un ricco pavimento.
E' lombi entrati mi son nella peccia,
e fo del cul per contrapeso groppa,   10
e' passi senza gli occhi muovo invano.
Dinanzi mi s'allunga la corteccia,
e per piegarsi adietro si ragroppa,
e tendomi com'arco soriano.
            Però fallace e strano   15
surge il iudizio che la mente porta,
ché mal si tra' per cerbottana torta.
            La mia pittura morta
difendi orma', Giovanni, e 'l mio onore,
non sendo in loco bon, né io pittore.   20

1*

The garland on her golden hair, cheerful and finely woven with flowers, is so joyful that each flower presses the one in front as if all are vying to be the first to kiss her head!

That dress which fits tightly round her breast, and then seems to flow down freely, is happy as the day is long, and that net made of what is called spun-gold never tires of touching her cheeks and neck.

But that happy ribbon of fine gold thread seems to rejoice more fully still, being so arranged that it presses and touches the bosom it encircles.

And the simple girdle that twines round her seems to be saying to itself: 'Here I wish to clasp forever.' So what then might my arms do?

(Sonnet, *c.* 1507)

2*

In this difficult position I've given myself a goitre – as does the water to the peasants of Lombardy, or anyway of some country or another – for it shoves my stomach up to hang beneath my chin.

My beard points to heaven, and I feel the nape of my neck on my hump; I bend my breast like a harpy's, and, with its non-stop dripping from above, my brush makes my face a richly decorated floor.

My loins have gone up into my belly, and I make my backside into a croup as a counterweight; and I cannot see where to put my feet.

In front my hide is stretched, and behind the curve makes it wrinkled, as I bend myself like a Syrian bow.

So the thoughts that arise in my mind are false and strange, for one shoots badly through a crooked barrel.

Defend my dead painting from now on, Giovanni, and my honour, for I am not well placed, nor indeed a painter.

(Tailed sonnet, for Giovanni da Pistoia, 1509–10)

3

Signor, se vero è alcun proverbio antico,
questo è ben quel, che chi può mai non vuole.
Tu hai creduto a favole e parole
e premiato chi è del ver nimico.
I' sono e fui già tuo buon servo antico,   5
a te son dato come e' raggi al sole,
e del mie tempo non ti incresce o dole,
e men ti piaccio se più m'affatico.
Già sperai ascender per la tua altezza,
e 'l giusto peso e la potente spada   10
fussi al bisogno, e non la voce d'ecco.
Ma 'l cielo è quel c'ogni virtù disprezza
locarla al mondo, se vuol c'altri vada
a prender frutto d'un arbor ch'è secco.

4

Qua si fa elmi di calici e spade
e 'l sangue di Cristo si vend'a giumelle,
e croce e spine son lance e rotelle,
e pur da Cristo paziïenzia cade.
Ma non ci arrivi più 'n queste contrade,   5
ché n'andre' 'l sangue suo 'nsin alle stelle,
poscia c'a Roma gli vendon la pelle,
e ècci d'ogni ben chiuso le strade.
S'i' ebbi ma' voglia a perder tesauro,
per ciò che qua opra da me è partita,   10
può quel nel manto che Medusa in Mauro;
ma se alto in cielo è povertà gradita,
qual fia di nostro stato il gran restauro,
s'un altro segno ammorza l'altra vita?

5

Tu ha' 'l viso più dolce che la sapa,
e passato vi par sù la lumaca,
tanto ben lustra, e più bel c'una rapa;
e' denti bianchi come pastinaca,

3*

Lord, if any ancient proverb is true it is surely this: he who can never wants to. You have believed tales and talk, and rewarded those who are the enemies of truth.

I am and ever was your good and faithful servant, I have been as united to you as rays to the sun; and yet you do not feel concern or compassion for the time I've given, and I please you less the more hard work I do.

I once hoped to rise thanks to your high state, but what I needed was the just scales and the powerful sword, not to hear my own voice echo.

But it is heaven itself that disdains to find a place on earth for any virtue, if it asks men to go and take fruit from a withered tree.

(Sonnet, probably c. 1511)

4*

Here from chalices helmets and swords are made; the blood of Christ is sold by the bucketful; his cross and thorns are lances and shields – and still Christ shows patience.

But let him not come to us again in these parts, for his blood would spurt right up to the stars, since in Rome his skin is sold, and here the way is barred to any good.

If I ever had a wish to lose treasure, now is the time, since here work has been taken from me, and he who wears the mantle* can do what Medusa did in Mauritania;*

but if high in heaven poverty is pleasing, who will bring about the great restoration of our state, if another standard* kills that other life?

(Sonnet, probably for Giovanni da Pistoia, probably 1512)

5*

You have a face sweeter than must,* and a snail seems to have passed across it, it shines so much, and it is more beautiful than a turnip; teeth white as parsnips, so that you would charm even the pope; and eyes the colour of theriac;* and hair whiter and blonder

in modo tal che invaghiresti 'l papa;   5
e gli occhi del color dell'utriaca;
e' cape' bianchi e biondi più che porri:
ond'io morrò, se tu non mi soccorri.

    La tua bellezza par molto più bella
che uomo che dipinto in chiesa sia: 10
la bocca tua mi par una scarsella
di fagiuo' piena, sì come'è la mia;
le ciglia paion tinte alla padella
e torte più c'un arco di Sorìa;
le gote ha' rosse e bianche, quando stacci,   15
come fra cacio fresco e' rosolacci.

    Quand'io ti veggo, in su ciascuna poppa
mi paion duo cocomer in un sacco,
ond'io m'accendo tutto come stoppa,
bench'io sia dalla zappa rotto e stracco.   20
Pensa: s'avessi ancor la bella coppa,
ti seguirrei fra l'altre me' c'un bracco:
dunche s'i massi aver fussi possibile,
io fare' oggi qui cose incredibile.

6

    Chiunche nasce a morte arriva
nel fuggir del tempo; e 'l sole
niuna cosa lascia viva.
Manca il dolce e quel che dole
e gl'ingegni e le parole;   5
e le nostre antiche prole
al sole ombre, al vento un fummo.
Come voi uomini fummo,
lieti e tristi, come siete;
e or siàn, come vedete,   10
terra al sol, di vita priva.
        Ogni cosa a morte arriva.
Già fur gli occhi nostri interi
con la luce in ogni speco;
or son voti, orrendi e neri,   15
e ciò porta il tempo seco.

than leeks: so I shall die if you do not come to my help.

Your beauty seems much more beautiful even than people painted in churches: your mouth seems to me a bag full of beans, as mine is; your eyebrows seem dyed by smoke from a frying pan and more bent than a Syrian bow;* when you are sifting flour, your cheeks are white and red, like poppies among fresh cheese.

When I look at you, those breasts of yours seem to me like two watermelons in a sack, and so I am all on fire like tow, even though I'm broken and tired out by the hoe. Believe me: if I still had the cup of beauty, I'd follow you through the other women better than a hound; so if it were possible for me to have blocks of stone, I'd here today make incredible things.

(Three octaves, 1518–24, possibly 1523)

6

Whoever is born arrives at death through time's swift passage; and the sun leaves nothing alive. They disappear – what is sweet and what brings pain, man's thoughts and words; and our ancient lineages are as shadows to the sun, smoke to the wind. Like you, we were men, happy and sad as you are; but now we are, as you see, dust in the sun, deprived of life.

Everything arrives at death. Once our eyes were fully formed, shining in both sockets; now these are empty, horrible and black: such is the work of time.

(*Barzelletta* or *frottola*, before 1524)

7

Quand'il servo il signor d'aspra catena
senz'altra speme in carcer tien legato,
volge in tal uso el suo stato,
che libertà domanderebbe appena.

E el tigre e 'l serpe ancor l'uso raffrena,   5
e 'l fier leon ne' folti boschi nato;
e 'l nuovo artista, all'opre affaticato,
coll'uso del sudor doppia suo lena.

Ma 'l foco a tal figura non s'unisce;
ché se l'umor d'un verde legno estinge,   10
il freddo vecchio scalda e po' 'l nutrisce,

e tanto il torna in verde etate e spinge,
rinnuova e 'nfiamma, allegra e 'ngiovanisce,
c'amor col fiato l'alma e 'l cor gli cinge.

E se motteggia o finge,   15
chi dice in vecchia etate esser vergogna
amar cosa divina, è gran menzogna.

L'anima che non sogna,
non pecca amar le cose di natura,
usando peso, termine e misura.   20

8

Vivo al peccato, a me morendo vivo;
vita già mia non son, ma del peccato:
mie ben dal ciel, mie mal da me m'è dato,
dal mie sciolto voler, di ch'io son privo.

Serva mie libertà, mortal mie divo   5
a me s'è fatto. O infelice stato!
a che miseria, a che viver son nato!

9

La vita del mie amor non è 'l cor mio,
c'amor di quel ch'i' t'amo è senza core;
dov'è cosa mortal, piena d'errore,
esser non può già ma', né pensier rio.

Amor nel dipartir l'alma da Dio   5

7

When a lord holds his servant bound in prison, with harsh chains and devoid of any hope, that servant becomes so accustomed to his wretched state that he would scarcely ask for freedom.

And custom tames even the tiger and the serpent, and the fierce lion born in leafy wood; and the young artist, tired by work, on becoming accustomed to sweat redoubles his vigour.

But fire does not conform to such a pattern: for though it consumes the moisture of a green piece of wood, it heats the cold old one and then nourishes him,

and finally returns and propels him back to his green age, renews and inflames him, brings him joy and youthfulness, for with its breath love twines around his heart and soul.

And if anyone jeers or pretends otherwise, saying that in old age it is shameful to love something divine, this is a great lie.

The soul that does not dream commits no sin in loving the things of nature, if it does so with balance, restraint and measure.

(Tailed sonnet, c. 1524–8)

8

I live to sin, to kill myself I live; no longer is my life my own, but sin's; my good is given to me by heaven, my evil by myself, by my free will, of which I am deprived.

My freedom has made itself a slave, my mortal part has made itself a god for me. O unhappy state! to such misery, to such a life was I born!

(Partial sonnet, c. 1525)

9*

My love does not live in my heart, for the love with which I love you does not belong to the heart: such love can never be found where there is anything mortal and full of error, or evil thoughts.

In sending down our souls from God, Love gave me a clear eye

me fe' san occhio e te luc' e splendore;
né può non rivederlo in quel che more
di te, per nostro mal, mie gran desio.
    Come dal foco el caldo, esser diviso
non può dal bell'etterno ogni mie stima,   10
ch'exalta, ond'ella vien, chi più 'l somiglia.
    Poi che negli occhi ha' tutto 'l paradiso,
per ritornar là dov'i' t'ama' prima,
ricorro ardendo sott'alle tuo ciglia.

10

In me la morte, in te la vita mia;
tu distingui e concedi e parti el tempo;
quante vuo', breve e lungo è 'l viver mio.
    Felice son nella tuo cortesia.
Beata l'alma, ove non corre tempo,   5
per te s'è fatta a contemplare Dio.

11

    Quanta dolcezza al cor per gli occhi porta
quel che 'n un punto el tempo e morte fura!
Che è questo però che mi conforta
e negli affanni cresce e sempre dura.
    Amor, come virtù viva e accorta,   5
desta gli spirti ed è più degna cura.
Risponde a me: – Come persona morta
mena suo vita chi è da me sicura. –
    Amore è un concetto di bellezza
immaginata o vista dentro al core,   10
amica di virtute e gentilezza.

12

    Del fiero colpo e del pungente strale
la medicina era passarmi 'l core;
ma questo è propio sol del mie signore,
crescer la vita dove cresce 'l male.
    E se 'l primo suo colpo fu mortale,   5

and you light and splendour; and so my great desire* cannot but see God again in that part of you which, to our misfortune, dies.

My discerning power itself can no more be separated from the eternal beauty* than can heat from fire; it exalts whoever most resembles him from whom it comes.

Since in your eyes you have paradise entire, in order to return to where I first loved you, I hasten burning to find myself again under your eyes.

(Sonnet, *c.* 1526)

10*

In me is death, in you my life; you determine, allot and parcel out time; as you wish, my life will be short or long.

I am happy according as you are kind. Blessed is the soul, where time does not run; through you it is formed to contemplate God.

(Partial sonnet, 1520s)

11

What sweetness he brings to the heart through the eyes who in an instant bears off time and death! He it is, then, who comforts me, and in times of trial gains in strength and remains always with me.

Love, as a power that brings life and wisdom, awakens our spirits and is most worth our concern. He answers me: 'Whoever is immune to me leads his life like one who is dead.'

Love is a concept born of beauty that is imagined or seen in the heart, and that is a friend of virtue and graciousness.*

(Partial sonnet, 1520s)

12

The remedy for the savage blow from the piercing arrow would be for it to pass through my heart; but this power belongs to my lord alone, to increase life where hurt increases.

And if his first blow was fatal, with it came at the same time a messenger from Love who said to me: 'Love, indeed burn; for mortal

seco un messo di par venne d'Amore
che mi disse: – Ama, anz'ardi; ché chi muore
non ha da gire al ciel nel mondo altr'ale.
    I' son colui che ne' prim'anni tuoi
gli occhi tuo infermi volsi alla beltate   10
che dalla terra al ciel vivo conduce. –

13

    Spirto ben nato, in cu' si specchia e vede
nelle tuo belle membra oneste e care
quante natura e 'l ciel tra no' può fare,
quand'a null'altra suo bell'opra cede:
    spirto leggiadro, in cu' si spera e crede   5
dentro, come di fuor nel viso appare,
amor, pietà, mercè, cose sì rare,
che ma' furn'in beltà con tanta fede:
    l'amor mi prende e la beltà mi lega;
la pietà, la mercè con dolci sguardi   10
ferma speranz' al cor par che ne doni.
    Qual uso o qual governo al mondo niega,
qual crudeltà per tempo o qual più tardi,
c'a sì bell'opra morte non perdoni?

14

    Dimmi di grazia, Amor, se gli occhi mei
veggono 'l ver della beltà c'aspiro,
o s'io l'ho dentro allor che, dov'io miro,
veggio scolpito el viso di costei.
    Tu 'l de' saper, po' che tu vien con lei   5
a torm'ogni mie pace, ond'io m'adiro;
né vorre' manco un minimo sospiro,
né men ardente foco chiederei.
    – La beltà che tu vedi è ben da quella,
ma cresce poi c'a miglior loco sale,   10
se per gli occhi mortali all'alma corre.
    Quivi si fa divina, onesta e bella,
com'a sé simil vuol cosa immortale:
questa e non quella agli occhi tuo precorre. –

beings have in this world no other wings with which to rise to heaven.

'I am he who in your early years turned your weak eyes to beauty, which leads those still alive from earth to heaven.'

(Partial sonnet, 1520s)

13*

Well-born spirit, in whose beautiful limbs, graceful and dear, one sees reflected how much nature and the heavens can achieve among us when they yield to no other beautiful work of theirs:

lovely spirit, within whom one confidently hopes to find what outwardly appears in your face – love, compassion, kindness, qualities so rare that they have never before been found so closely linked to beauty:

love takes me, and beauty binds me; compassion and kindness in sweet glances seem to give my heart firm hope.

What pattern or law on earth, what cruelty whether swift or slow, would prevent death from sparing a work so beautiful?

(Sonnet, after 1528)

14

'Tell me in your kindness, Love, if my eyes do really see the beauty that I long for;* or whether this is rather within me, since, wherever I gaze, I see as if sculpted that woman's face.

'You must know, because you come with her to take from me all my peace, which makes me angry; and yet I would not wish to lose the slightest sigh, nor would I ask for a fire that burned less fiercely.'

'The beauty that you see does indeed come from her, but it grows once it has risen to a better place,* when through mortal eyes it speeds to the soul.

'There it becomes divine, virtuous and beautiful, since an immortal being wishes all else to be like itself:* it is this beauty not that other which goes before your eyes.'

(Sonnet, after 1528)

15

Se 'l mie rozzo martello i duri sassi
forma d'uman aspetto or questo or quello,
dal ministro che 'l guida, iscorge e tiello,
prendendo il moto, va con gli altrui passi.

Ma quel divin che in cielo alberga e stassi,   5
altri, e sé più, col propio andar fa bello;
e se nessun martel senza martello
si può far, da quel vivo ogni altro fassi.

E perché 'l colpo è di valor più pieno
quant'alza più se stesso alla fucina,   10
sopra 'l mie questo al ciel n'è gito a volo.

Onde a me non finito verrà meno,
s'or non gli dà la fabbrica divina
aiuto a farlo, c'al mondo era solo.

16

Come fiamma più cresce più contesa
dal vento, ogni virtù che 'l cielo esalta
tanto più splende quant'è più offesa.

17

Amor, la tuo beltà non è mortale:
nessun volto fra noi è che pareggi
l'immagine del cor, che 'nfiammi e reggi
con altro foco e muovi con altr'ale.

18

Oilmè, oilmè, ch'i' son tradito
da' giorni mie fugaci e dallo specchio
che 'l ver dice a ciascun che fiso 'l guarda!
Così n'avvien, chi troppo al fin ritarda,
com'ho fatt'io, che 'l tempo m'è fuggito: 5

15*

If my rough hammer, in shaping the hard stones into the form of this or that human appearance, derives its motion from the master who guides, directs and sustains it, then it moves as another would have it do.

But that divine hammer, which lodges and abides in heaven, with its own movement makes others beautiful, and all the more itself;* and if no hammer can be made without a hammer, then every other hammer is made from that living one.

And since every blow is of greater strength the higher the hammer is raised at the forge, this one has flown to heaven above mine.

So mine will remain unfinished for me, if the divine smith will not now give help to make it to him who was on earth my only help.

(Sonnet, *c.* 1528)

16

As a flame grows stronger the more it is buffeted by the wind, every virtue that heaven exalts shines more brightly the more it is attacked.

(Tercet, after *c.* 1528)

17

Love, your beauty is not mortal: there is no face among us can match the image in the heart, which you inflame and rule with another fire, and move with other wings.

(Quatrain, *c.* 1530)

18

Alas, alas, I have been betrayed by my fleeting days and by the mirror that tells the truth to everyone who looks steadily into it! This is what happens to anyone who too long puts off thinking about his end, as I have done, while time has slipped me by: like me, he suddenly finds himself old. And I cannot repent, nor do I prepare

si trova come me 'n un giorno vecchio.
Né mi posso pentir, né m'apparecchio,
né mi consiglio con la morte appresso.
Nemico di me stesso,
inutilmente i pianti e' sospir verso,   10
ché non è danno pari al tempo perso.
    Oilmè, oilmè, pur riterando
vo 'l mio passato tempo e non ritruovo
in tutto un giorno che sie stato mio!
Le fallace speranze e 'l van desio,   15
piangendo, amando, ardendo e sospirando
(c'affetto alcun mortal non m'è più nuovo)
m'hanno tenuto, ond'il conosco e pruovo,
lontan certo dal vero.
Or con periglio pèro;   20
ché 'l breve tempo m'è venuto manco,
né sarie ancor, se s'allungassi, stanco.
    I' vo lasso, oilmè, né so ben dove;
anzi temo, ch'il veggio, e 'l tempo andato
mel mostra, né mi val che gli occhi chiuda.   25
Or che 'l tempo la scorza cangia e muda,
la morte e l'alma insieme ognor fan pruove,
la prima e la seconda, del mie stato.
E s'io non sono errato
(che Dio 'l voglia ch'io sia),   30
l'etterna pena mia
nel mal libero inteso oprato vero
veggio, Signor, né so quel ch'io mi spero.

19

    Se l'immortal desio, c'alza e corregge
gli altrui pensier, traessi e' mie di fore,
forse c'ancor nella casa d'Amore
farie pietoso chi spietato regge.
    Ma perché l'alma per divina legge   5
ha lunga vita, e 'l corpo in breve muore,
non può 'l senso suo lode o suo valore
appien descriver quel c'appien non legge.
    Dunche, oilmè! come sarà udita

myself, nor reconsider my ways, even with death near. My own worst enemy, I uselessly pour out tears and sighs, for there is no harm to equal that of wasted time.

Alas, alas, though I keep going over my past life, I do not find a single day that has been my own! False hopes and vain desire have kept me weeping, loving, burning and sighing (for no mortal emotion is a stranger to me now), as I well know and daily prove again, far indeed from the true good. Now in danger I perish: time's short passage has run out for me, and even if it were to lengthen I should not tire of my ways.

I go wearily on, alas, yet without really knowing where; or rather I fear I do, for I see where, and my past shows this to me, and it does me no good to close my eyes. Now that time is changing skin and moult, death and my soul are locked in battle every hour, one against the other, for my final state. And if I am not mistaken (God grant that I may be), I see the eternal punishment due for my having, in freedom, badly understood and acted on the truth, Lord; nor do I know what I may hope for.

(*Canzone* of three stanzas, *c.* 1530)

19

If desire of the immortal, which raises and directs men's thoughts aright, were to make mine show clearly, that would perhaps make merciful him who rules without mercy still in the realm of Love.

But since by divine law the soul has a long life, while the body after a short time dies, the senses cannot fully tell the soul's praise or worth, since this they cannot fully perceive.

Alas, then, how shall the chaste desire which sets aflame my heart within be heard by those who always see themselves in others?

la casta voglia che 'l cor dentro incende   10
da chi sempre se stesso in altrui vede?
    La mie cara giornata m'è impedita
col mie signor c'alle menzogne attende,
c'a dire il ver, bugiardo è che nol crede.

20

    S'un casto amor, s'una pietà superna,
s'una fortuna infra dua amanti equale,
s'un'aspra sorte all'un dell'altro cale,
s'un spirto, s'un voler duo cor governa;
    s'un'anima in duo corpi è fatta etterna,   5
ambo levando al cielo e con pari ale;
s'Amor d'un colpo e d'un dorato strale
le viscer di duo petti arda e discerna;
    s'amar l'un l'altra e nessun se medesmo,
d'un gusto e d'un diletto, a tal mercede   10
c'a un fin voglia l'uno e l'altro porre:
    se mille e mille, non sarien centesmo
a tal nodo d'amore, a tanta fede;
e sol l'isdegno il può rompere e sciorre.

21

    Tu sa' ch'i' so, signor mie, che tu sai
ch'i' vengo per goderti più da presso,
e sai ch'i' so che tu sa' ch'i' son desso:
a che più indugio a salutarci omai?
    Se vera è la speranza che mi dai,   5
se vero è 'l gran desio che m'è concesso,
rompasi il mur fra l'uno e l'altra messo,
ché doppia forza hann' i celati guai.
    S'i' amo sol di te, signor mie caro,
quel che di te più ami, non ti sdegni,   10
ché l'un dell'altro spirto s'innamora.
    Quel che nel tuo bel volto bramo e 'mparo,
e mal compres' è dagli umani ingegni,
chi 'l vuol saper convien che prima mora.

I am shut off from the dear company of my lord who pays heed to falsehoods, while, if truth be told, he is a liar who does not believe it.

(Sonnet, probably for Tommaso Cavalieri, late 1532 or after)

20

If one chaste love, if one sublime compassion, if one fortune affects two lovers equally, if one harsh fate matters as much to both, if one spirit, if one will rules two hearts;

if one soul in two bodies is made eternal, lifting both to heaven and with the same wings; if Love with one blow and with one golden arrow burns and tests the bowels in two bosoms;

if each loves the other, and neither himself, with one taste and with one delight, with this reward that both direct their will to the one end;

if these were multiplied a thousand times and more, they would not make a hundredth part of such a bond of love, and of such great faithfulness; and only disdain can break and dissolve it.

(Sonnet, for Tommaso Cavalieri, late 1532 or after)

21

You know that I know, my lord, that you know that I come here to enjoy you nearer at hand, and you know that I know that you know who I really am: why then this hesitation to greet each other, even now?

If the hope that you give me is true, if the great desire that has been granted me is true, let the wall raised up between these two be broken down, for hidden difficulties have a double force.

If in you, my dear lord, I love only what you most love in yourself,* do not be disdainful, for it is simply one spirit loving the other.

What I long for and discover in your lovely face, and what is badly understood by human minds – whoever would know this must first die.

(Sonnet, for Tommaso Cavalieri, late 1532 or after)

22

S'i' avessi creduto al primo sguardo
di quest'alma fenice al caldo sole
rinnovarmi per foco, come suole
nell'ultima vecchiezza, ond'io tutt'ardo,
    qual più veloce cervio o lince o pardo   5
segue 'l suo bene e fugge quel che dole,
agli atti, al riso, all'oneste parole
sarie cors'anzi, ond'or son presto e tardo.
    Ma perché più dolermi, po' ch'i' veggio
negli occhi di quest'angel lieto e solo   10
mie pace, mie riposa e mie salute?
    Forse che prima sarie stato il peggio
vederlo, udirlo, s'or di pari a volo
seco m'impenna a seguir suo virtute.

23

Sol pur col foco il fabbro il ferro stende
al concetto suo caro e bel lavoro,
né senza foco alcuno artista l'oro
al sommo grado suo raffìna e rende;
    né l'unica fenice sé riprende   5
se non prim'arsa; ond'io, s'ardendo moro,
spero più chiar resurger tra coloro
che morte accresce e 'l tempo non offende.
    Del foco, di ch'i' parlo, ho gran ventura
c'ancor per rinnovarmi abbi in me loco,   10
sendo già quasi nel numer de' morti.
    O ver, s'al cielo ascende per natura,
al suo elemento, e ch'io converso in foco
sie, come fie che seco non mi porti?

24

Sì amico al freddo sasso è 'l foco interno
che, di quel tratto, se lo circumscrive,
che l'arda e spezzi, in qualche modo vive,
legando con sé gli altri in loco etterno.

22

If I had believed that at the first sight of this dear phoenix in the hot sun I should renew myself through fire, as does that bird in its extreme old age, a fire in which my whole being burns,

then as the swiftest deer or lynx or leopard seeks its good and flees what does it harm, I should before this have run to his actions, smile and virtuous words, where now I am eager but slow.

But why go on lamenting, since I see in the eyes of this happy angel alone my peace, my rest and my salvation?

Perhaps it would have been for the worse to have seen and heard him before, if he now gives me wings like his to fly with him, following where his virtue leads.

(Sonnet, for Tommaso Cavalieri, late 1532 or after)

23

It is only with fire that a smith can shape iron into a beautiful and cherished work in accordance with his concept, and without fire no craftsman can refine his gold and bring it to the highest quality;

nor can the unique phoenix recover life unless it first be burned; likewise, if I die by burning, I hope to rise again to a purer life among those whom death enriches and time no longer harms.

It is my good fortune that the fire of which I speak has even now taken hold in me to renew me, when I am already almost numbered among the dead.

How can it be, then, if fire by nature ascends to the heavens,* to its proper sphere, and I am turned to fire, that it does not carry me upwards along with it?

(Sonnet, probably for Tommaso Cavalieri, late 1507 or after)‡[1]

24

So friendly to the cold stone is the fire within it that if, when drawn forth from it, the fire so surrounds it that it burns and breaks

---

[1] On the significance of the double dagger at the end of some of the notes, see above, pp. xviii–xix.

E se 'n fornace dura, istate e verno   5
vince, e 'n più pregio che prima s'ascrive,
come purgata infra l'altre alte e dive
alma nel ciel tornasse da l'inferno.
    Così tratto di me, se mi dissolve
il foco, che m'è dentro occulto gioco,   10
arso e po' spento aver più vita posso.
    Dunche, s'i' vivo, fatto fummo e polve,
etterno ben sarò, s'induro al foco;
da tale oro e non ferro son percosso.

25

Forse perché d'altrui pietà mi vegna,
perché dell'altrui colpe più non rida,
nel mie propio valor, senz'altra guida,
caduta è l'alma che fu già sì degna.
    Né so qual militar sott'altra insegna   5
non che da vincer, da campar più fida,
sie che 'l tumulto dell'avverse strida
non pèra, ove 'l poter tuo non sostegna.
    O carne, o sangue, o legno, o doglia strema,
giusto per vo' si facci el mie peccato,   10
di ch'i' pur nacqui, e tal fu 'l padre mio.
    Tu sol se' buon; la tuo pietà suprema
soccorra al mie preditto iniquo stato,
sì presso a morte e sì lontan da Dio.

26

Se nel volto per gli occhi il cor si vede,
altra segno non ho più manifesto
della mie fiamma; addunche basti or questo,
signor mie caro, a domandar mercede.
    Forse lo spirto tuo, con maggior fede   5
ch'i' non credo, che sguarda il foco onesto
che m'arde, fie di me pietoso e presto,

it, the stone lives on in a certain way, binding with its substance other stones into an eternal place.

And if it survives in the furnace, it will defeat summer and winter, and become more highly prized than formerly, like a soul which after being purged takes its place among the other noble and divine souls, having returned to heaven from hell.*

Likewise, if the fire that plays secretly within me when once drawn forth dissolves me, I then, though burned to the point of being spent, may have a fuller life.

So if, reduced to smoke and dust, I live after enduring in the fire, I shall indeed be eternal: it is by gold, then, not by iron that I am struck.

(Sonnet, of uncertain date)‡

25

Perhaps it is to make me have pity on others, to make me no longer laugh at others' faults, that, relying on my own strength, looking to no other guide, my soul has fallen that was once so worthy.

I know no other standard under which to fight that will give greater hope, not of victory but of escape, so that the tumult of the hostile shouts may not cause me to perish, where your power does not sustain me.

O flesh, O blood, O wood, O utmost pain, may you atone for my sin,* in which I was born, as was my father before me.

You alone are good; may your supreme mercy come to the help of this evil state of mine, so close to death and yet so far from God.

(Sonnet, c. 1533)

26

Since a person's heart is seen in his face through his eyes, I have no other sign that more clearly shows the flame within me; so now let this be enough, my sweet lord, to ask for mercy.

Perhaps your spirit, responding more warmly than I dare believe, when it sees the virtuous fire that burns me, will take pity on me and draw near, just as grace abounds for those who truly ask for it.

Happy will that day be when it comes, as it surely must! May time

come grazia c'abbonda a chi ben chiede.
    O felice quel dì, se questo è certo!
Fermisi in un momento il tempo e l'ore,   10
il giorno e 'l sol nella su' antica traccia;
    acciò ch'i' abbi, e non già per mie merto,
il desïato mie dolce signore
per sempre nell'indegne e pronte braccia.

27

Non so se s'è la desïata luce
del suo primo fattor, che l'alma sente,
o se dalla memoria della gente
alcun'altra beltà nel cor traluce;
    o se fama o se sogno alcun produce   5
agli occhi manifesto, al cor presente,
di sé lasciando un non so che cocente
ch'è forse or quel c'a pianger mi conduce.
    Quel ch'i' sento e ch'i' cerco e chi mi guidi
meco non è; né so ben veder dove   10
trovar mel possa, e par c'altri mel mostri.
    Questo, signor, m'avvien, po' ch'i' vi vidi,
c'un dolce amaro, un sì e no mi muove:
certo saranno stati gli occhi vostri.

28

Se 'l foco fusse alla bellezza equale
degli occhi vostri, che da que' parte,
non avrie 'l mondo sì gelata parte
che non ardessi com'acceso strale.
    Ma 'l ciel, pietoso d'ogni nostro male,   5
a noi d'ogni beltà, che 'n voi comparte,
la visiva virtù toglie e diparte
per tranquillar la vita aspr'e mortale.
    Non è par dunche il foco alla beltate,
ché sol di quel s'infiamma e s'innamora   10
altri del bel del ciel, ch'è da lui inteso.
    Così n'avvien, signore, in questa etate:

and the passing hours stop at that very moment, and the day, and the sun in its ancient course,

so that I may have, though not through any merit of mine, my sweet, longed-for lord forever in my unworthy and yet ready arms.*

(Sonnet, for Tommaso Cavalieri, probably early 1533)

27

I do not know if it is the very longed-for light of the one who first made it that my soul feels; or if some other beauty lodged in my memory of people shines in my heart;

or if flame or dreaming brings someone before my eyes, or makes him present in my heart, leaving behind a burning trace I cannot describe – perhaps it is this which draws my heart to tears.

What I feel and what I seek, and who may guide me to it, lie beyond my power; and I cannot clearly see where I may find it, though it seems that someone may show me.

This, lord, is what has happened to me from the time I saw you: something bitter and sweet, a yes and no move me: it is certainly your eyes that have brought this about.

(Sonnet, probably for Tommaso Cavalieri in its final version, 1533–42/6)

28

If the fire that springs from your eyes were equal to their beauty, the world would have no part so frozen that it would not burn like a flaming arrow.

But heaven, merciful towards our every ill, blocks and distances our power to see from the entire beauty that it has lavished on you, to make peaceful our harsh and mortal life.

My fire is not, then, equal to that beauty, for men are inflamed by and fall in love with only that part of heaven's beauty which they can understand.

This is what happens to me, lord, at this age: if it does not seem to you that for you I burn and die, my slight ability is the cause of my weak flame.

(Sonnet, very probably for Tommaso Cavalieri, probably mid 1533)

se non vi par per voi ch'i' arda e mora,
poca capacità m'ha poco acceso.

29

Dal dolce pianto al doloroso riso,
da una etterna a una corta pace
caduto son: là dove 'l ver si tace,
soprasta 'l senso a quel da lui diviso.
   Né so se dal mie core o dal tuo viso   5
la colpa vien del mal, che men dispiace
quante più cresce, o dall'ardente face
de gli occhi tuo rubati al paradiso.
   La tuo beltà non è cosa mortale,
ma fatta su dal ciel fra noi divina;   10
ond'io perdendo ardendo mi conforto,
   c'appresso a te non esser posso tale.
Se l'arme il ciel del mie morir destina,
chi può, s'i' muoio, dir c'abbiate il torto?

30

Felice spirto, che con zelo ardente,
vecchio alla morte, in vita il mio cor tieni,
e fra mill'altri tuo diletti e beni
me sol saluti fra più nobil gente;
   come mi fusti agli occhi, or alla mente,   5
per l'altru' fiate a consolar mi vieni,
onde la speme il duol par che raffreni,
che non men che 'l disio l'anima sente.
   Dunche, trovando in te chi per me parla
grazia di te per me fra tante cure,   10
tal grazia ne ringrazia chi ti scrive.
   Che sconcia e grande usur saria a farla,
donandoti turpissime pitture
per rïaver persone belle e vive.

29

From sweet lament to suffering smile, from an eternal to a passing peace have I fallen: for when the truth keeps silent in someone, the senses, cut off from the truth, dominate in him.

And I do not know what is to be blamed for the evil which displeases less the more it grows: whether my heart, or your face, or the burning light of your eyes stolen from paradise.

Your beauty is no mortal thing, but something divine among us made in heaven above; so when the burning overwhelms me I comfort myself

that near you I could not be otherwise. If heaven destines the weapons to bring about my death, who could say, if I should die, that the fault were yours?

(Sonnet, probably for Tommaso Cavalieri, c. 1533)

30

Happy spirit, who, with eager burning, keep alive my heart which old age turns towards death, and, among the thousand other delights and blessings you bring, greet me alone among more noble people;

as once to my eyes so now to my mind you come to give a consolation others cannot offer; and so hope seems to curb the suffering which my soul feels no less than desire.

Since, then, he who speaks for me* finds in you a graciousness towards me among your many concerns, he who writes to you thanks you for such graciousness.

For it would be vile usury on a grand scale were I to give you pictures of the basest kind,* and in return receive most beautiful and living people.

(Sonnet, for Tommaso Cavalieri, c. 1533)

31

I' mi credetti, il primo giorno ch'io
mira' tante bellezze uniche e sole,
fermar gli occhi com'aquila nel sole
nella minor di tante ch'i' desio.

Po' conosciut'ho il fallo e l'erro mio: 5
ché chi senz'ale un angel seguir vole,
il seme a' sassi, al vento le parole
indarno isparge, e l'intelletto a Dio.

Dunche, s'appresso il cor non mi sopporta
l'infinita beltà che gli occhi abbaglia,   10
né di lontan par m'assicuri o fidi,

che fie di me? qual guida o qual scorta
fie che con teco ma' mi giovi o vaglia,
s'appresso m'ardi e nel partir m'uccidi?

32

Non posso altra figura immaginarmi
o di nud'ombra o di terrestre spoglia,
col più alto pensier, tal che mie voglia
contra la tuo beltà di quella s'armi.

Ché da te mosso, tanto scender parmi,   5
c'Amor d'ogni valor mi priva e spoglia,
ond'a pensar di minuir mie doglia
duplicando, la morte viene a darmi.

Però non val che più sproni mie fuga,
doppiando 'l corso alla beltà nemica,   10
ché 'l men dal più veloce non si scosta.

Amor con le sue man gli occhi m'asciuga,
promettendomi cara ogni fatica;
ché vile esser non può chi tanto costa.

33

Veggio nel tuo bel viso, signor mio,
quel che narrar mal puossi in questa vita;
l'anima, della carne ancor vestita,

31

On the day that I first gazed on so many unique, singular beauties, I thought I should be able to fix my eyes, like the eagle on the sun, on the least of the many I desire.

Then I recognized my fault and error: for if someone who lacked wings wished to pursue an angel, this would be as useless as throwing seeds on stones, words on the wind, and the intellect on God.*

If, then, when near, the infinite beauty that dazzles my eyes does not allow my heart to bear up, and from afar seems not to reassure me or give me confidence,

what will become of me? What guide or escort can there be who in regard of you will ever give me help or strength, if you, when near, burn me, and, by parting, kill me?

(Sonnet, very probably for Tommaso Cavalieri, c. 1533)

32

Not even by raising my thoughts as high as possible can I imagine another figure, whether of pure spirit or of earthly flesh, with which my will may arm itself against your beauty.

For, separated from you, I seem to sink so low that Love deprives and strips me of all strength; so when I think of lessening my sufferings he, doubling them, threatens me with death.

It is useless, then, for me to spur on my flight, doubling the pace at which I fly from hostile beauty, for the less speedy never gains distance on one who moves more swiftly.

Love with his own hands dries my eyes, promising that I shall hold all effort dear: for he who costs so much cannot himself be base.

(Sonnet, for Tommaso Cavalieri, c. 1534)

33

I see in your beautiful face, my lord, what in this life words cannot well describe; with it my soul, still clothed in flesh, has already often risen to God.

con esso è già più volte ascesa a Dio.

   E se 'l vulgo malvagio, isciocco e rio,   5
di quel che sente, altrui segna e addita,
non è l'intensa voglia men gradita,
l'amor, la fede e l'onesto desio.

   A quel pietoso fonte, onde siàn tutti,
s'assembra ogni beltà che qua si vede   10
più c'altra cosa alle persone accorte;

   né altro saggio abbiàn né altri frutti
del cielo in terra; e chi v'ama con fede
transcende a Dio e fa dolce la morte.

34

   Sì come nella penna e nell'inchiostro
è l'alto e 'l basso e 'l medïocre stile,
e ne' marmi l'immagin ricca e vile,
secondo che 'l sa trar l'ingegno nostro;

   così, signor mie car, nel petto vostro,   5
quante l'orgoglio è forse ogni atto umile;
ma io sol quel c'a me propio è e simile
ne traggo, come fuor nel viso mostro.

   Chi semina sospir, lacrime e doglie,
(l'umor dal ciel terreste, schietto e solo,   10
a vari semi vario si converte),

   però pianto e dolor ne miete e coglie;
chi mira alta beltà con sì gran duolo,
ne ritra' doglie e pene acerbe e certe.

35

   Com'io ebbi la vostra, signor mio,
cercand'andai fra tutti e' cardinali
e diss'a tre da vostra part' addio.

   Al Medico maggior de' nostri mali
mostrai la detta, onde ne rise tanto   5
che 'l naso fe' dua parti dell'occhiali.

   Il servito da voi pregiat' e santo
costà e qua, sì come voi scrivete,

And if the common people, evil, stupid and base as they are, attribute and assign to others only what they themselves can feel, my intense longing is no less cherished for that, nor my love, faithfulness and virtuous desire.

To those who are wise, nothing more resembles that merciful spring whence all derive than every beauty to be found here;

nor have we any other sign or other fruits of heaven on earth; and he who loves you faithfully rises to God above and holds death sweet.

(Sonnet, for Tommaso Cavalieri, *c.* 1534)

34

Just as in pen and ink there lie all styles from high to low, and, in marble, images rich and feeble, according as our mind knows how to bring each forth;

so, my dear lord, in your breast there perhaps may lie as much as pride an attitude of complete humility; but from it I bring forth only what characterizes and resembles me, as my face shows clearly.

The moisture which from the heavens descends to earth, though in itself unmixed and of a single kind, is differently transformed by different seeds; so, too, whoever sows sighs, tears and suffering

reaps and gathers from them lament and pain; and whoever gazes on high beauty with so much pain draws forth from it suffering and sorrow sharp and sure.

(Sonnet, for Tommaso Cavalieri, *c.* 1534)

35*

When I received your letter, my lord, I went searching among all the cardinals and gave greetings on your behalf to the three.

To the greatest Doctor* of our ills I showed what you had written, and he laughed at it so much that his nose split his glasses in two.

He who, as you say, is served by you* both there and here, a man greatly esteemed and saintly, was so pleased by it that he laughed just as much.

I have not yet shown it to him who holds* the closest secrets of

n'ebbe piacer, che ne ris'altro tanto.

A quel che tien le cose più secrete   10
del Medico minor non l'ho ancor visto;
farebbes'anche a lui, se fusse prete.

Ècci molt'atri che rinegon Cristo
che voi non siate qua; né dà lor noia,
ché chi non crede si tien manco tristo.   15

Di voi a tutti caverò la foia
di questa vostra; e chi non si contenta
affogar possa per le man del boia.

La Carne, che nel sal si purg' e stenta,
che saria buon per carbonat' ancora,   20
di voi più che di sé par si rammenta.

Il nostro Buonarroto, che v'adora,
visto la vostra, se ben veggio, parmi
c'al ciel si lievi mille volte ogn'ora;

e dice che la vita de' sua marmi   25
non basta a far il vostro nom' eterno,
come lui fanno i divin vostri carmi.

Ai qual non nuoce né state né verno,
dal temp' esenti e da morte crudele,
che fama di virtù non ha in governo.   30

E come vostro amico e mio fedele
disse: – Ai dipinti, visti i versi belli,
s'appiccon voti e s'accendon candele.

Dunque i' son pur nel numero di quelli,
da un goffo pittor senza valore   35
cavato a' pennell' e alberelli.

Il Bernia ringraziate per mio amore,
che fra tanti lui sol conosc' il vero
di me; ché chi mi stim' è 'n grand'errore.

Ma la sua disciplin' el lum' intero   40
mi può ben dar, e gran miracol fia,
a far un uom dipint' un uom da vero. –

Così mi disse; e io per cortesia
vel raccomando quanto so e posso,
che fia l'apportator di questa mia.   45

Mentre la scrivo a vers'a verso, rosso
diveng'assai, pensando a chi la mando,

the lesser Doctor; what you say would apply to him, if he were a priest.

There are many others who would deny Christ to have you here; this would not do them any harm, for whoever does not believe is regarded as less of a rogue.

Through this letter I'll take away from everyone the passion to see you, and if anyone is not content with that he can be drowned at the hands of the executioner.

The Meat,* which is purged and hardened in salt, and which would also be tasty if done over coals, seems to have you more in mind than himself.

Our Buonarroti, who adores you, having seen your letter, seems to me, if my eyesight isn't faulty, to be raised to heaven a thousand times every hour;

and he says that the life he gives to his marbles would not be enough to make your name eternal, as your divine songs do his.

These will be harmed neither by summer nor by winter, being exempt from time and cruel death, which has no power over fame based on virtue.*

And as your faithful friend and mine, he said, after seeing your beautiful lines: 'Votive offerings* are hung in front of painted figures and candles are lit there.

'So I am certainly among such figures, but one of no value, brought forth by a clumsy painter from his brushes and pots.

'Thank Berni with my love, for he alone among so many knows what I am really like, for anyone who has a high opinion of me is badly mistaken.

'But his teaching can certainly bring me to the true light; and it will be a great miracle to make a painted man a real one.'

This is what he said to me; and I beg leave to commend him to you as much as I possibly can; he will be the bearer of this letter.

As I write it line by line I become quite red, thinking of the one I'm sending it to, for my poetry is rough and clumsy, not that of a professional.

None the less, I commend myself likewise to you; there is nothing else of note; I am always and ever yours.

To you who are numbered among life's special gifts I offer myself wholly; and do not think that I would ever fail you, even if I were to lose my cowl.*

send' il mio non professo, goffo e grosso.
    Pur nondimen così mi raccomando
anch'io a voi, e altro non accade;   50
d'ogni tempo son vostro e d'ogni quando.
    A voi nel numer delle cose rade
tutto mi v'offerisco, e non pensate
ch'i' manchi, se 'l cappuccio non mi cade.
    Così vi dico e giuro, e certo siate,   55
ch'i' non farei per me quel che per voi:
e non m'abbiat'a schifo come frate.
    Comandatemi, e fate poi da voi.

36

    Vorrei voler, Signor, quel ch'io non voglio:
tra 'l foco e 'l cor di ghiaccia un vel s'asconde
che 'l foco ammorza, onde non corrisponde
la penna all'opre, e fa bugiardo 'l foglio.
    I' t'amo con la lingua, e poi mi doglio   5
c'amor non giunge al cor; né so ben onde
apra l'uscio alla grazia che s'infonde
nel cor, che scacci ogni spietato orgoglio.
    Squarcia 'l vel tu, Signor, rompi quel muro
che con la suo durezza ne ritarda   10
il sol della tuo luce, al mondo spenta!
    Manda 'l preditto lume a noi venturo,
alla tuo bella sposa, acciò ch'io arda
il cor senz'alcun dubbio, e te sole senta.

37

    Sento d'un foco un freddo aspetto acceso
che lontan m'arde e sé con seco agghiaccia;
pruovo una forza in due leggiadre braccia
che muove senza moto ogni altro peso.
    Unico spirto e da me solo inteso,   5
che non ha morte e morte altrui procaccia,
veggio e truovo chi, sciolto, 'l cor m'allaccia,
e da chi giova sol mi sento offeso.

So I say and swear to you, and you may rest assured, that I would not do for myself what I would do for you: and do not despise me because I am a friar.

Command me, and then do as you wish.

(*Capitolo*, for Francesco Berni, late 1533 or early 1534)

36

I should like to will, Lord, what I do not will: between the fire and my heart lies hidden a veil of ice that quenches the fire, and so my pen does not correspond to my actions, and the paper is made a liar.

I love you with my tongue, and then I grieve that love does not reach my heart; and yet I am completely at a loss to know how I may open the door to grace, that it may pour into my heart and drive out all unfeeling pride.

Tear you, Lord, the veil, break down that wall which with its hardness keeps from us the light of your sun, now quenched in the world!

Send that light, promised to come to us one day, to your lovely spouse,* so that my heart may burn free from all doubt, and feel you alone.

(Sonnet, probably *c.* 1534)

37

I feel a cold face lit by a fire that burns me from afar, yet in itself is freezing; I sense in two lovely arms a power that itself unmoved moves every other weight.

I see a unique spirit understood by me alone, who is himself untouched by death yet causes death in others, and find one who, himself free, holds my heart bound; and by one who offers only help, I feel myself harmed.

How can it be, lord, if one can scarcely give to others what one

Com'esser può, signor, che d'un bel volto
ne porti 'l mio così contrari effetti,   10
se mal può chi non gli ha donar altrui?
    Onde al mio viver lieto, che m'ha tolto,
fa forse come 'l sol, se nol permetti,
che scalda 'l mondo e non è caldo lui.

38

Veggio co' be' vostr'occhi un dolce lume
che co' mie ciechi già veder non posso;
porto co' vostri piedi un pondo addosso,
che de' mie zoppi non è già costume.
    Volo con le vostr'ale senza piume;   5
col vostro ingegno al ciel sempre son mosso;
dal vostro arbitrio son pallido e rosso,
freddo al sol, caldo alle più fredde brume.
    Nel voler vostro è sol la voglia mia,
i miei pensier nel vostro cor si fanno,   10
nel vostro fiato son le mie parole.
    Come luna da sé sol par ch'io sia,
ché gli occhi nostri in ciel veder non sanno
se non quel tanto che n'accende il sole.

39

I' mi son caro assai più ch'i' non soglio;
poi ch'i' t'ebbi nel cor più di me vaglio,
come pietra c'aggiuntovi l'intaglio
è di più pregio che 'l suo primo scoglio.
    O come scritta o pinta carta o foglio   5
più si riguarda d'ogni straccio o taglio,
tal di me fo, da po' ch'i' fu' berzaglio
segnato dal tuo viso, e non mi doglio.
    Sicur con tale stampa in ogni loco
vo, come quel c'ha incanti o arme seco,   10
c'ogni periglio gli fan venir meno.
    I' vaglio contr'a l'acqua e contr'al foco,
col segno tuo rallumino ogni cieco,
e col mie sputo sano ogni veleno.

does not oneself possess, that from a beautiful face mine should draw such opposite effects?

So as regards my joy in life, which it has taken from me, your face perhaps acts (unless you prevent it) as does the sun, which heats the world yet is not hot itself.

(Sonnet, for Tommaso Cavalieri, c. 1532–4)‡

38

With your beautiful eyes I see a sweet light which with my blind eyes I certainly cannot see; with your feet I carry on my back a weight which my lame feet certainly could not bear.

Though lacking feathers I fly with your wings; with your mind I am always carried to heaven; on your decision turns whether I am pale or red, cold in the sun, warm in the coldest mists.

In your will alone does my will consist, my thoughts spring from your heart, with your breath are my words formed.

On my own I seem like the moon left to itself, for our eyes can see nothing whatever in the heavens except what is lit up by the sun.

(Sonnet, for Tommaso Cavalieri, c. 1534)‡

39

I am much dearer to myself than I ever used to be; since I have had you in my heart I value myself more, as a stone once worked on is more highly prized than it was as a raw block.

Or as a page once written on or a sheet when painted is considered of greater worth than any crumpled or torn-off piece, so I consider myself since I became a target marked by your face; and I have no regrets.

Nowhere do I fear to go bearing such an image, like one possessing charms or arms, that make every danger fade before him.

I am proof against water and against fire, with your mark I restore light to all the blind, and with my spittle I cure every poison.*

(Sonnet, probably for Tommaso Cavalieri, probably c. 1534)‡

40

Spargendo il senso il troppo ardor cocente
fuor del tuo bello, in alcun altro volto,
men forza ha, signor, molto
qual per più rami alpestro e fier torrente.
Il cor, che del più ardente   5
foco più vive, mal s'accorda allora
co' rari pianti e men caldi sospiri.
L'alma all'error presente
gode c'un di lor mora
per gire al ciel, là dove par c'aspiri.   10
La ragione i martiri
fra lor comparte; e fra più salde tempre
s'accordan tutt'a quattro amarti sempre.

41

D'altrui pietoso e sol di sé spietato
nasce un vil bruto, che con pena e doglia
l'altrui man veste e la suo scorza spoglia
e sol per morte si può dir ben nato.
    Così volesse al mie signor mie fato   5
vestir suo viva di mie morta spoglia,
che, come serpe al sasso si discoglia,
pur per morte potria cangiar mie stato.
    O fussi sol la mie l'irsuta pelle
che, del suo pel contesta, fa tal gonna   10
che con ventura stringe sì bel seno,
    ch'i' l'are' pure il giorno; o le pianelle
che fanno a quel di lor basa e colonna,
ch'i' pur ne porterei duo nevi almeno.

42

Al cor di zolfo, a la carne di stoppa,
a l'ossa che di secco legno sièno;
a l'alma senza guida e senza freno
al desir pronto, a la vaghezza troppa;
    a la cieca ragion debile e zoppa   5

40

When the senses spread their excessive, searing heat by going beyond your beautiful face to others', its force is greatly lessened, like a wild mountain torrent when it spreads into several branches. The heart, which draws most life from the most fiercely burning fire, then feels ill at ease with the rare laments and the cooler sighs. The soul, conscious of the error, rejoices that one of them dies down, thus allowing the soul to go to heaven, to where it seems to aspire. Reason divides the torments equally among them; and with each in a steadier state, all four agree among themselves to love you always.

(Madrigal, probably for Tommaso Cavalieri, probably 1534–6, revised 1546)‡

41*

A lowly worm is born considerate of others and inconsiderate only of itself: with pain and suffering it sheds its own covering and clothes another's hand, and may really be said to be born only in order to die.

Would that my destiny wished the same for me as regards my lord: that I might clothe his living skin with my dead skin, so that, as a serpent sloughs on a stone, I might through death change my condition.

O might my skin alone be the hairy skin that, woven from its own skin, makes the gown whose good fortune it is to bind so lovely a breast,

so that I should have it at least in daytime; or might I be the slippers which make themselves a base and support for him, that I might at the very least carry him for two winters.

(Sonnet, probably for Tommaso Cavalieri, *c.* 1535)

42

If one's heart is made of sulphur, one's skin of tow, one's bones of dry wood; if one's soul is without guide and without rein for its ready desire and its excessive attraction;

if one's reason is blind, weak and lamed by the birdlime and the snares of which the world is full; it is little wonder that one should in

al vischio, a' lacci di che 'l mondo è pieno;
non è gran maraviglia, in un baleno
arder nel primo foco che s'intoppa.
    A la bell'arte che, se dal ciel seco
ciascun la porta, vince la natura,   10
quantunche sé ben prema in ogni loco;
    s'i' nacqui a quella né sordo né cieco,
proporzionato a chi 'l cor m'arde e fura,
colpa è di chi m'ha destinato al foco.

43

    A che più debb'i' omai l'intensa voglia
sfogar con pianti o con parole meste,
se di tal sorte 'l ciel, che l'alma veste,
tard' o per tempo alcun mai non ne spoglia?
    A che 'l cor lass' a più languir m'invoglia,   5
s'altri pur dee morir? Dunche per queste
luci l'ore del fin fian men moleste;
c'ogni altro ben val men c'ogni mia doglia.
    Però se 'l colpo ch'io ne rub' e 'nvolo
schifar non posso, almen, s'è destinato,   10
chi entrerà 'nfra la dolcezza e 'l duolo?
    Se vint' e preso i' debb'esser beato,
maraviglia non è se nudo e solo
resto prigion d'un cavalier armato.

44

    O notte, o dolce tempo, benché nero,
con pace ogn' opra sempr' al fin assalta;
ben vede e ben intende chi t'esalta,
e chi t'onor' ha l'intelletto intero.
    Tu mozzi e tronchi ogni stanco pensiero   5
ché l'umid' ombra ogni quiet' appalta,
e dall'infima parte alla più alta
in sogno spesso porti, ov'ire spero.
    O ombra del morir, per cui si ferma

a flash be burned up by the first fire one comes across.

If to the art of beauty which conquers nature, if anyone brings it with him from heaven, even though nature strives well everywhere,*

if to that art I was born neither deaf nor blind, responsive then to whoever burns and steals my heart, this is the fault of the one who has destined me to the fire.

(Sonnet, for Tommaso Cavalieri, 1534–8 or later)‡

43

What point is there in my still giving vent to my intense emotion in weeping or sad words, if heaven, which clothes the soul, neither late nor early rescues one from such a fate?

What point is there in my tired heart's driving me more and more to pine away, if all must surely die? The final hours will be less troubling to my eyes, knowing that no good whatever is worth all my suffering.

So if I cannot avoid the blow which I steal and rob from him, since it is in fact destined, who will enter there where sweetness wars with pain?

If it is only by being overcome and taken that I may be happy, then it is not to be wondered at if defenceless and alone I remain the prisoner of an armed cavalier.*

(Sonnet, for Tommaso Cavalieri, of uncertain date, but probably 1534–8 or later)

44

O night, O sweet time, although black, all work finally struggles to an end and reaches peace; whoever exalts you sees clearly and clearly understands, and whoever honours you is of sound mind.

You break and cut off all tired thoughts, for your soft shadow offers complete rest, and in dreams you often carry one from the lowest to the highest sphere, where I hope to go.

O shadow of death, through which is ended every misery hostile to man's soul and heart, last of man's afflictions and their true remedy:

ogni miseria a l'alma, al cor nemica,   10
ultimo delli afflitti e buon rimedio;
   tu rendi sana nostra carn' inferma,
rasciughi i pianti e posi ogni fatica,
e furi a chi ben vive ogn'ira e tedio.

45

Colui che fece, e non di cosa alcuna,
il tempo, che non era anzi a nessuno,
ne fe' d'un due e diè 'l sol alto all'uno,
all'altro assai più presso diè la luna.
   Onde 'l caso, la sorte e la fortuna   5
in un momento nacquer dì ciascuno;
e a me consegnaro il tempo bruno,
come a simil nel parto e nella cuna.
   E come quel che contrafà se stesso,
quando è ben notte, più buio esser suole,   10
ond'io di far ben mal m'affliggo e lagno.
   Pur mi consola assai l'esser concesso
far giorno chiar mia oscura notte al sole
che a voi fu dato al nascer per compagno.

46

Non vider gli occhi miei cosa mortale
allor che ne' bei vostri intera pace
trovai, ma dentro, ov'ogni mal dispiace,
chi d'amor l'alma a sé simil m'assale;
   e se creata a Dio non fusse equale,   5
altro che 'l bel di fuor, c'agli occhi piace,
più non vorria; ma perch'è si fallace,
transcende nella forma universale.
   Io dico c'a chi vive quel che muore
quetar non può disir; né par s'aspetti   10
l'eterno al tempo, ove altri cangia il pelo.
   Voglia sfrenata el senso è, non amore,
che l'alma uccide; e 'l nostro fa perfetti
gli amici qui, ma più per morte in cielo.

you restore health to our sick flesh, dry away our tears and bring all toil to rest; and you banish from those who live rightly all anger and frustration.

(Sonnet, possibly for Tommaso Cavalieri, 1535–46, possibly 1545)

45

He who, from nothing whatever, made time, which did not exist before all else, divided it in two: to one part he gave the high sun, to the other the moon, which is much nearer.

From these were born the chance, condition and fortune of every individual; to me they assigned the dark time, as being similar to me at birth and in the cradle.

Just as night as it advances grows ever darker, so I grow more like myself in being ever more evil, which troubles me and grieves me.

Yet it consoles me greatly that to change my dark night into bright day has been granted to the sun which was given to you at birth as your companion.

(Sonnet, probably for Tommaso Cavalieri, c. 1535–46, possibly 1545)‡

46

It was not something mortal my eyes saw when in your beautiful eyes I found complete peace; rather, they saw within, where all evil displeases, him who* assails my soul, similar to himself, with love;

if my soul had not been created by God equal to himself,* then indeed it would wish for nothing more than external beauty, which pleases the eyes; but because this is so deceptive, the soul rises above to beauty's universal form.*

I declare that what dies cannot satisfy the desire of one who lives; nor likewise should one look for the eternal in time, where man's body grows old.

To the senses belongs not love but unbridled desire, which kills the soul; but our love makes our friendships perfect here, and even more beyond death in paradise.

(Sonnet, probably for Tommaso Cavalieri, c. 1535–46)

47

Per ritornar là donde venne fora,
l'immortal forma al tuo carcer terreno
venne com'angel di pietà sì pieno,
che sana ogn'intelletto e 'l mondo onora.

Questo sol m'arde e questo m'innamora,   5
non pur di fuora il tuo volto sereno:
c'amor non già di cosa che vien meno
tien ferma speme, in cui virtù dimora.

Né altro avvien di cose altere e nuove
in cui si preme la natura, e 'l cielo   10
è c'a' lor parti largo s'apparecchia;

né Dio, suo grazia, mi si mostra altrove
più che 'n alcun leggiadro e mortal velo;
e quel sol amo perch'in lui si specchia.

48

Gli occhi mie vaghi delle cose belle
e l'alma insieme della suo salute
non hanno altra virtute
c'ascenda al ciel, che mirar tutte quelle.
Dalle più alte stelle   5
discende uno splendore
che 'l desir tira a quelle,
e qui si chiama amore.
Né altro ha il gentil core
che l'innamori e arda, e che 'l consigli,   10
c'un volto che negli occhi lor somigli.

49

Io dico a voi c'al mondo avete dato
l'anima e 'l corpo e lo spirto 'nsïeme:
in questa cassa oscura è 'l vostro lato.

50

S'egli è, donna, che puoi

47

In order to return to the place from which it came, the immortal form came to your earthly prison like an angel so full of mercy that it heals every intellect and brings honour to the world.

This alone inflames me and calls forth my love, not something merely external, your bright face: love in which virtue dwells certainly does not place firm hope in what passes away.

This is what happens to all excellent and rare beings which nature labours to produce, and which heaven generously endows at their birth;

but God, in his graciousness, does not show himself more fully to me elsewhere than in some lovely, mortal veil;* and I love that solely because in it He is reflected.

(Sonnet, for Tommaso Cavalieri, 1536–42, revised 1546)‡

48

My eyes, eager for beautiful things, and my soul no less for its salvation, have no other means by which they may ascend to heaven than to gaze on all such things. From the highest stars descends a shining light which draws our desire to them: this we here call love. The noble heart has nothing else that can make it love and burn, nothing else to guide it, than a face which in its eyes acts as those stars do.

(Madrigal, possibly for Tommaso Cavalieri, 1534–46)‡

49*

I say to you who have given to the world your whole selves – body, soul and spirit: you will end up in this dark coffin.

(Tercet, 1534–5 or later)

50*

If it is true, lady, that though divine in beauty you can act like

come cosa mortal, benché sia diva
di beltà, c'ancor viva
e mangi e dorma e parli qui fra noi,
a non seguirti poi,   5
cessato il dubbio, tuo grazia e mercede,
qual pena a tal peccato degna fora?
Ché alcun ne' pensier suoi,
co' l'occhio che non vede,
per virtù propia tardi s'innamora   10
Disegna in me di fuora,
com'io fo in pietra od in candido foglio,
che nulla ha dentro, e èvvi ciò ch'io voglio.

51

S'egli è che 'l buon desio
porti dal mondo a Dio
alcuna cosa bella,
sol la mie donna è quella,
a chi ha gli occhi fatti com'ho io.   5
Ogni altra cosa oblio
e sol di tant'ho cura.
Non è gran maraviglia,
s'io l'amo e bramo e chiamo a tutte l'ore;
né propio valor mio,   10
se l'alma per natura
s'appoggia a chi somiglia
ne gli occhi gli occhi, ond'ella scende fore.
Se sente il primo amore
come suo fin, per quel qua questa onora: 15
c'amar diè 'l servo chi 'l signore adora.

52

Non pur la morte, ma 'l timor di quella
da donna iniqua e bella,
c'ognor m'ancide, mi difende e scampa;
e se talor m'avvampa
più che l'usato il foco in ch'io son corso,   5
non trovo altro soccorso

any mortal being, who still lives and eats and sleeps and speaks here among us, then not to follow you when, thanks to your grace and mercy, all doubt on this has ceased – what punishment* would be sufficient for such a sin? For anyone who relies on his own thoughts, using the eye that does not see,* is slow to love through his own power. Form in me a shape from outside, as I do in stone or on a blank sheet, which in itself contains nothing, and then has there what I wish.

(Madrigal, for Vittoria Colonna, *c.* 1536)

51

If it is true that something beautiful may carry good desire from the world to God, that can be only my lady, for one whose eyes have been fashioned as have mine. I forget all else, and care for her alone. It is no great wonder if I love and long for her, and call to her all the time; nor is mine the merit if my soul by its very nature rests on her who resembles in her eyes those eyes from which it first came forth. And if my soul feels the first love* as its end, it is for that end's sake that it honours her here: for whoever adores the lord must love his servant.

(Madrigal, possibly for Vittoria Colonna, 1536–46)‡

52

Not just death itself but the very fear of it defends and rescues me from an evil but beautiful woman, who at every moment kills me; and if sometimes the fire into which I have fallen burns me with a more searing heat than usual, I find no other help than death's firm image deep in my heart: for where death is there Love will not approach.

(Madrigal, for 'the beautiful and cruel lady',* 1536–46)‡

che l'immagin sua ferma in mezzo il core:
ché dove è morte non s'appressa Amore.

53

Mentre che 'l mie passato m'è presente,
sì come ognor mi viene,
o mondo falso, allor conosco bene
l'errore e 'l danno dell'umana gente:
quel cor, c'alfin consente   5
a' tuo lusinghi e a' tuo van diletti,
procaccia all'alma dolorosi guai.
Ben lo sa chi lo sente,
come spesso prometti
altrui la pace e 'l ben che tu non hai   10
né debbi aver già mai.
Dunche ha men grazia chi più qua soggiorna:
ché chi men vive più lieve al ciel torna.

54

Condotto da molt'anni all'ultim'ore,
tardi conosco, o mondo, i tuo diletti:
la pace che non hai altrui prometti
e quel riposo c'anzi al nascer muore.
La vergogna e 'l timore   5
degli anni, c'or prescrive
il ciel, non mi rinnuova
che 'l vecchio e dolce errore,
nel qual chi troppo vive
l'anima 'ncide e nulla al corpo giova.   10
Il dico e so per pruova
di me, che 'n ciel quel sol ha miglior sorte
ch'ebbe al suo parto più presso la morte.

55

– Beati voi che su nel ciel godete
le lacrime che 'l mondo non ristora,
favvi amor forza ancora,

53

While my past is present to me, as continually happens, I then, O false world, recognize full well the error of the human race and the harm this causes: the heart which finally gives in to your enticements and to your empty pleasures brings to the soul painful troubles. He knows this well who experiences it: how you often promise men the peace and the good that you do not have, nor ever ought to have. So he has the lesser grace whose stay is longer here: for whoever lives less long returns to heaven more lightly.

(Madrigal, 1536–46)‡

54

Brought by many years to my last hours, too late, O world, I recognize your delights for what they are: you promise men a peace which you do not have and that repose which dies before it is born. The shame and fear that come with old age, which heaven now ordains for me, serve only to renew in me the old, sweet error, by which he who lives too long kills the soul and brings no benefit to the body. This I declare, and know the truth of it from what I have undergone, that in heaven only he has the happier state who at his birth had death closer to him.

(Madrigal, 1536–46)‡

55

'O happy you who in heaven above enjoy the reward of tears to which this world pays no heed, does love still have power over you, or are you instead freed from it by death?'

o pur per morte liberi ne siete?
– La nostra etterna quiete,   5
fuor d'ogni tempo, è priva
d'invidia, amando, e d'angosciosi pianti.
– Dunche a mal pro' ch'i' viva
convien, come vedete,
per amare e servire in dolor tanti.   10
Se 'l cielo è degli amanti
amico, e 'l mondo ingrato,
amando, a che son nato?
A viver molto? E questo mi spaventa:
ché 'l poco è troppo a chi ben serve e stenta.   15

                                    56

In più leggiadra e men pietosa spoglia
altr'anima non tiene
che la tuo, donna, il moto e 'l dolce anelo;
tal c'alla ingrata voglia
al don di tuo beltà perpetue pene   5
più si convien c'al mie soffrire 'l cielo.
I' nol dico e nol celo
s'i' bramo o no come 'l tuo 'l mie peccato,
ché, se non vivo, morto ove te sia,
o, te pietosa, che dove beato   10
mi fa 'l martir, si' etterna pace mia.
Se dolce mi saria
l'inferno teco, in ciel dunche che fora?
Beato a doppio allora
sare' a godere i' sol nel divin coro   15
quel Dio che 'n cielo e quel che 'n terra adoro.

                                    57

Non men gran grazia, donna, che gran doglia
ancide alcun, che 'l furto a morte mena,
privo di speme e ghiacciato ogni vena,
se vien subito scampo che 'l discioglia.
    Simil se tuo mercé, piú che ma' soglia,   5

'Our eternal rest, entirely beyond time, is, though we love, unmarked by envy or by anguished tears.'

'It is my misfortune, then, that, as you can see, I must live to love and serve with such great sufferings. If to lovers heaven is friendly and the world uncaring, why, since I love, was I born? To live long? But it is this which terrifies me: for even a short life is too much for anyone who serves well and goes unrewarded.'

(Madrigal, 1536–46)‡

56

No soul, lady, moves and sweetly breathes in a covering more beautiful and less merciful than yours, and so your ungrateful attitude to the gift of your beauty deserves eternal pains more than my suffering does heaven. I neither declare nor deny whether I desire to be a sinner like you, so that if not when alive then when dead I may be with you; or whether, if you become merciful, you may be my eternal peace where my martyrdom will make me blessed. If with you hell would be sweet for me, what then might my state be in heaven? I should then be doubly blessed, for I alone in the divine choir would enjoy both that God in heaven and that god on earth whom I adore.

(Madrigal, for 'the beautiful and cruel lady', 1536–46)‡

57

Great grace, lady, no less than great suffering can kill a thief being led to death, devoid of hope and paralysed in every vein, if the pardon granting him freedom is suddenly presented.

Likewise if your mercy, bestowed more generously than ever before on this misery of mine so full of woes, should with excessive

nella miseria mie d'affanni piena,
con superchia pietà mi rasserena,
par, più che 'l pianger, la vita mi toglia.
    Così n'avvien di novell'aspra o dolce:
ne' lor contrari è morte in un momento,   10
onde s'allarga o troppo stringe 'l core.
    Tal tuo beltà, c'Amore e 'l ciel qui folce,
se mi vuol vivo affreni il gran contento,
c'al don superchio debil virtù muore.

58

Non ha l'ottimo artista alcun concetto
c'un marmo solo in sé non circonscriva
col suo superchio, e solo a quello arriva
la man che ubbidisce all'intelletto.
    Il mal ch'io fuggo, e 'l ben ch'io mi prometto,   5
in te, donna leggiadra, altera e diva,
tal si nasconde; e perch'io più non viva,
contraria ho l'arte al disïato effetto.
    Amor dunque non ha, né tua beltate
o durezza o fortuna o gran disdegno,   10
del mio mal colpa, o mio destino o sorte;
    se dentro del tuo cor morte e pietate
porti in un tempo, e che 'l mio basso ingegno
non sappia, ardendo, trarne altro che morte.

59

Sì come per levar, donna, si pone
in pietra alpestra e dura
una viva figura,
che là più cresce u' più la pietra scema;
tal alcun'opre buone,   5
per l'alma che pur trema,
cela il superchio della propria carne
co' l'inculta sua cruda e dura scorza.
Tu pur dalle mie streme
parti puo' sol levarne,   10

compassion bring me peace, then it seems that this would take away not just my tears but life itself.

Such is what happens to us with harsh or sweet news: contrary though they be, both result in instant death, by causing the heart to expand or to contract too much.

And so your beauty, nourished here by Love and heaven, should restrain the great happiness it brings if it would have me live: for touched by an excessive gift a weak power dies.

(Sonnet, very probably for Vittoria Colonna, probably late 1530s)‡

58

The greatest artist does not have any concept which a single piece of marble does not itself contain within its excess, though only a hand that obeys the intellect can discover it.

The evil which I flee, and the good to which I aspire, gracious, noble and divine lady, lie hidden in you in just this way; but that I may not live hereafter, my art brings about the opposite of what I desire.

It is not Love, then, nor your beauty, nor harshness, nor fortune, nor haughty disdain that is to be blamed for my evil, nor my destiny nor fate,

if within your heart you carry at the same time death and mercy, and my low mind, in its burning, does not know how to draw forth from it anything but death.

(Sonnet, for Vittoria Colonna, 1538–41/4)

59

Just as, lady, it is by removing that one places in hard, alpine stone a living figure, which grows greater precisely where the stone grows less, so the excess that is one's own flesh, with its coarse, rough, hard bark, hides some good works in the soul which trembles under this burden. You alone can so remove from my outer being,* for in me there is regarding me neither will nor strength.

(Madrigal, for Vittoria Colonna, 1538–41/4)

ch'in me non è di me voler né forza.

60

Non pur d'argento o d'oro
vinto dal foco esser po' piena aspetta,
vota d'opra prefetta,
la forma, che sol fratta il tragge fora;
tal io, col foco ancora   5
d'amor dentro ristoro
il desir voto di beltà infinita,
di coste' ch'i' adoro,
anima e cor della mie fragil vita.
Alta donna e gradita   10
in me discende per sì brevi spazi,
c'a trarla fuor convien mi rompa e strazi.

61

Tanto sopra me stesso
mi fai, donna, salire,
che non ch'i' 'l possa dire,
nol so pensar, perch'io non son più desso.
Dunche, perché, più spesso,   5
se l'alie tuo mi presti,
non m'alzo e volo al tuo leggiadro viso,
e che con teco resti,
se dal ciel n'è concesso
ascender col mortale in paradiso?   10
Se non ch'i' sia diviso
dall'alma per tuo grazia, e che quest'una
fugga teco suo morte, è mie fortuna.

62

A l'alta tuo lucente dïadema
per la strada erta e lunga,
non è, donna, chi giunga,
s'umiltà non v'aggiugni e cortesia:
il montar cresce, e 'l mie valore scema,   5

60

It is not unique, the mould which, empty of the work of art, finally stands ready to be filled by silver or gold melted by fire, and then brings forth the work only by being sundered; I, also, through the fire of love, replenish the desire within me, empty of infinite beauty, with her whom I adore, soul and heart of my fragile life. This noble and dear lady descends into me through such narrow spaces* that, for her to be brought forth, I too must be broken and shattered.

(Madrigal, for Vittoria Colonna, 1538–41/4)‡

61

You make me rise so high above myself, lady, that it is not just my power of speech but thought itself that fails to grasp what happens, for I am no longer myself. Why, then, if you give me wings, do I not more often raise myself and fly to your lovely face; and why may I not remain with you, if heaven has granted us to ascend to paradise with our mortal body? Yet I do recognize that it is my good fortune that, through your grace, I should be separated from my soul, and that it alone, being with you, should escape its death.

(Madrigal, for Vittoria Colonna, 1538–41/4)‡

62

There is no one, lady, who may reach your high, shining crown by mounting the long, steep road, unless you also reach down to him with humility and kindness: the ascent steepens, my strength fails, and my breath gives out halfway along the road. That your beauty should indeed be so exalted seems to bring delight to my

e la lena mi manca a mezza via.
Che tuo beltà pur sia
superna, al cor par che diletto renda,
che d'ogni rara altezza è ghiotto e vago:
po' per gioir della tuo leggiadria   10
bramo pur che discenda
là dov'aggiungo. E 'n tal pensier m'appago,
se 'l tuo sdegno presago,
per basso amare e alto odiar tuo stato,
a te stessa perdona il mie peccato.   15

63

Per esser manco, alta signora, indegno
del don di vostra immensa cortesia,
prima, all'incontro a quella, usar la mia
con tutto il cor volse 'l mie basso ingegno.
    Ma visto poi, c'ascendere a quel segno   5
propio valor non è c'apra la via,
perdon domanda la mie audacia ria,
e del fallir più saggio ognor divegno.
    E veggio ben com'erra s'alcun crede
la grazia, che da voi divina piove,   10
pareggi l'opra mia caduca e frale.
    L'ingegno, l'arte, la memoria cede:
c'un don celeste non con mille pruove
pagar del suo può già chi è mortale.

64

S'alcun legato è pur dal piacer molto,
come da morte altrui tornare in vita,
qual cosa è che po' paghi tanta aita,
che renda il debitor libero e sciolto?
    E se pur fusse, ne sarebbe tolto   5
il soprastar d'una mercé infinita
al ben servito, onde sarie 'mpedita
da l'incontro servire, a quella volto.
    Dunche, per tener alta vostra grazia,

heart which longs eagerly for all that is rare and sublime; but then to enjoy your loveliness I also crave that you descend to where I may reach. And I content myself with this thought: that when your reproachful insight reveals my sin to you, of loving your state as low and hating it as high, you will pardon yourself for having been its cause.

(Madrigal, very probably for Vittoria Colonna, probably late 1530s or early 1540s)‡

63

To be less unworthy, high lady, of the gift of your immense courtesy, my lowly mind at first tried wholeheartedly to reciprocate in kind.

But having seen then that my own powers can make no headway towards ascending to such a goal, I ask pardon for my wicked boldness, and through that fault grow constantly wiser.

And I see clearly how wrong it is to believe that my fleeting and frail activity could match that divine grace which rains down from you.

Mind, skill and memory give way: for one still mortal cannot repay a heavenly gift from his own resources, not even if he tries a thousand times.

(Sonnet, for Vittoria Colonna, of uncertain date, possibly *c.* 1541)‡

64

If someone is truly bound to another through having received a great favour, such as being brought back to life from death, what could possibly so repay such help as to render the debtor discharged and free?

And even were this possible, it would take, from him who had served well, the continual care of an infinite mercy, since this cannot exist where service has been given in return.

So, lady, to keep your graciousness high above my state, I yearn only that there seem to be in me ingratitude rather than courtesy,

donna, sopra 'l mie stato, in me sol bramo   10
ingratitudin più che cortesia:
   ché dove l'un dell'altro al par si sazia,
non mi sare' signor quel che tant'amo:
ché 'n parità non cape signoria.

65

   Per qual mordace lima
discresce e manca ognor tuo stanca spoglia,
anima inferma? or quando fie ti scioglia
da quella il tempo, e torni ov'eri, in cielo,
candida e lieta prima,   5
deposto il periglioso e mortal velo?
C'ancor ch'i' cangi 'l pelo
per gli ultim'anni e corti,
cangiar non posso il vecchio mie antico uso,
che con più giorni più mi sforza e preme.   10
Amore, a te nol celo,
ch'i' porto invidia a' morti,
sbigottito e confuso,
sì di sé meco l'alma trema e teme.
Signor, nell'ore streme,   15
stendi ver' me le tuo pietose braccia,
tomm'a me stesso e famm'un che ti piaccia.

66

   Ora in sul destro, ora in sul manco piede
variando, cerco della mie salute.
Fra 'l vizio e la virtute
il cor confuso mi travaglia e stanca,
come chi 'l ciel non vede,   5
che per ogni sentier si perde e manca.
Porgo la carta bianca
a' vostri sacri inchiostri,
c'amor mi sganni e pietà 'l ver ne scriva:
che l'alma, de sé franca,   10
non pieghi agli error nostri

for if each of us were equally to satisfy the other, you whom I so love could not then be my lord: for in equality there is no place for lordship.

(Sonnet, for Vittoria Colonna, of uncertain date, possibly *c.* 1541)

65

What biting file makes your tired hide wear away and fail, weak soul? O when will time free you from it, so that, having laid aside your dangerous and mortal veil, you may return to heaven where you once were, pure and happy? For though I change my skin in these last, short years, I cannot change my old, habitual way of life, which with each passing day binds and oppresses me all the more. Love, I will not hide from you that in my frightened and confused state I bear envy towards the dead, so greatly does my soul while still with me fear and tremble for its fate. Lord, in my last hours, stretch out to me your merciful arms, take me from myself and make me one who is pleasing to you.

(Madrigal, for Vittoria Colonna, *c.* 1538–41)

66

Sometimes on my right foot, sometimes on my left,* shifting from one to the other, I go in search of my salvation. Moving between vice and virtue, my confused heart troubles and wearies me, like one who does not see heaven, which along every path becomes lost from view and disappears. I hold out a blank page for your sacred ink, that your love may show how I deceive myself and your compassion may there write the truth, so that my soul, made master of itself, may not bend to our errors what little of my life remains, and I may live less blindly. I beg to know from you, high and divine lady, whether in heaven the humble sinner will hold a lesser rank than he who is perfectly good.

(Madrigal, for Vittoria Colonna, *c.* 1538–41)‡

mie breve resto, e che men cieco viva.
Chieggio a voi, alta e diva
donna, saper se 'n ciel men grado tiene
l'umil peccato che 'l superchio bene.   15

67

Quante più fuggo e odio ognor me stesso,
tanto a te, donna, con verace speme
ricorro; e manco teme
l'alma di me, quant'a te son più presso.
A quel che 'l ciel promesso   5
m'ha nel tuo volto aspiro
e ne' begli occhi, pien d'ogni salute:
e ben m'accorgo spesso,
in quel c'ogni altri miro,
che gli occhi senza 'l cor non han virtute.   10
Luci già mai vedute!
né da vederle è men che 'l gran desio;
ché 'l veder raro è prossimo a l'oblio.

68

Per fido esemplo alla mia vocazione
nel parto mi fu data la bellezza,
che d'ambo l'arti m'è lucerna e specchio.
S'altro si pensa, è falsa opinione.
Questo sol l'occhio porta a quella altezza   5
c'a pingere e scolpir qui m'apparecchio.
S'e' giudizi temerari e sciocchi
al senso tiran la beltà, che muove
e porta al cielo ogni intelletto sano,
dal mortale al divin non vanno gli occhi   10
infermi, e fermi sempre pur là d'ove
ascender senza grazia è pensier vano.

69

Spargendo gran bellezza ardente foco
per mille cori accesi,

67

The more I flee and hate myself with each passing hour, the more, lady, I have recourse to you with lively hope; and my soul has less fear of me the closer I am to you. I aspire to what heaven has promised me in your face and in your beautiful eyes, full of all salvation; and I often realize clearly, from what I see in every other face, that the eyes without the heart possess no power. Lights never seen before! and see them I ought, no less than I greatly desire, for to see them rarely is to risk forgetting them.

(Madrigal, for Vittoria Colonna, *c.* 1538–44, probably 1541–4)‡

68

From birth I was given beauty as a faithful guide to my vocation; it is a light and mirror for me in both the arts.* If anyone thinks otherwise, he is quite mistaken. This alone carries the eye to those heights which here I set myself to paint and sculpt.

If those of rash and foolish judgement drag down beauty to the senses, though it moves and carries every healthy mind to heaven, let them realize that eyes that are infirm do not move from the mortal to the divine sphere, but remain forever firmly fixed there whence to think of rising without grace is a vain hope.

(Double sestet, for Vittoria Colonna, possibly 1541–4)

69

Great beauty that scatters burning fire over a thousand hearts is like a heavy weight which if it bears down on one man alone kills

come cosa è che pesi,
c'un solo ancide, a molti è lieve e poco.
Ma, chiuso in picciol loco,   5
s'il sasso dur calcina,
che l'acque poi il dissolvon 'n un momento,
come per pruova il sa chi 'l ver dicerne:
così d'una divina
de mille il foco ho drento   10
c'arso m'ha 'l cor nelle mie parte interne;
ma le lacrime etterne
se quel dissolvon già sì duro e forte,
fie me' null'esser c'arder senza morte.

70

Se dal cor lieto divien bello il volto,
dal tristo il brutto; e se donna aspra e bella
il fa, chi fie ma' quella
che non arda di me com'io di lei?
Po' c'a destinguer molto   5
dalla mie chiara stella
da bello a bel fur fatti gli occhi mei,
contr'a sé fa costei
non men crudel che spesso
dichi: – Dal cor mie smorto il volto viene.–   10
Che s'altri fa se stesso,
pingendo donna, in quella
che farà poi, se sconsolato il tiene?
Dunc'ambo n'arien bene
ritrarla col cor lieto e 'l viso asciutto: 15
sé farie bella e me non farie brutto.

71

La carne terra, e qui l'ossa mie, prive
de' lor begli occhi e del leggiadro aspetto,
fan fede a quel ch'i fu' grazia e diletto
in che carcer quaggiù l'anima vive.

him but if borne by many is easy and light. Yet just as fire when
enclosed in a small space reduces hard stone to lime which water
can then dissolve in an instant, as he can testify who has seen this
process in action, so I have within me the fire of a thousand lovers
for a divine woman which has burnt my heart in my innermost
parts; yet if my unceasing tears dissolve what was once so hard and
strong, it will be better to become nothing than to burn without
dying.

(Madrigal, possibly for 'the beautiful and cruel lady', 1536–46)‡

70

If one's face becomes beautiful from having a happy heart, and
ugly from a sad one; and if it is made to be the latter by a harsh and
beautiful woman, what woman is there who would not burn for me
as I for her? Since through the influence of my bright star my eyes
were so formed as to be able to distinguish clearly one beauty from
another, she acts no less cruelly towards herself in often making me
say: 'My downcast face comes from my heart.' For if an artist
represents himself in painting a woman, what will he represent in
painting her, if she keeps him disconsolate? So it would be for both
our good if while portraying her I could have a happy heart and dry
face: she would then make herself beautiful and not make me ugly.

(Madrigal, possibly for 'the beautiful and cruel lady', 1536–46)‡

71

My flesh, being earth, and my bones deprived here of their
beautiful eyes and lovely face, bear witness to him for whom I was a
grace and delight what a prison the soul lives in here below.

(Quatrain, first of a series of fifty epitaphs for Cecchino [Francesco] Bracci,
sent to Luigi del Riccio in the course of 1544)*

72

S'i' fu' già vivo, tu sol, pietra, il sai,
che qui mi serri, e s'alcun mi ricorda,
gli par sognar: sì morte è presta e 'ngorda,
che quel ch'è stato non par fusse mai.

73

A la terra la terra e l'alma al cielo
qui reso ha morte; a chi morto ancor m'ama
ha dato in guardia mie bellezza e fama,
ch'etterni in pietra il mie terrestre velo.

74

Col sol de' Bracci il sol della natura,
per sempre estinto, qui lo chiudo e serro:
morte l'ancise senza spada o ferro,
c'un fior di verno picciol vento il fura.

75

Non altrimenti contro a sé cammina
ch'i' mi facci alla morte,
chi è da giusta corte
tirato là dove l'alma il cor lassa;
tal m'è morte vicina,   5
salvo più lento el mie resto trapassa.
Né per questo mi lassa
Amor viver un'ora
fra duo perigli, ond'io mi dormo e veglio:
la speme umile e bassa   10
nell'un forte m'accora,
e l'altro parte m'arde, stanco e veglio.
Né so il men danno o 'l meglio:
ma pur più temo, Amor, che co' tuo sguardi
più presto ancide quante vien più tardi.   15

72

If I was ever alive you alone know it, O stone, who here enclose me, for if anyone remembers me he seems merely to be dreaming: so ready and greedy is death that what once was seems never to have been.

(See poem 71)

73

Here death has restored earth to earth and the soul to heaven; to his safe-keeping who loves me still though I am dread, death has given my beauty and renown, that he may immortalize in stone my earthly veil.

(See poem 71)

74

Here I enclose and lock away with the sun of the Bracci the sun of nature forever extinguished; death killed him without sword or steel, for it takes but a little wind to carry off a winter flower.

(See poem 71)

75

No more unwillingly does a man condemned by a court of justice walk to where the soul leaves the heart than I do to death; this is as close to me, except that the time that remains to me passes more slowly. But that does not make Love leave me in peace for a single hour between two dangers that threaten me, whether I wake or sleep: on the one hand my hope's being weak and scanty grieves me greatly; on the other Love burns me, old and weary though I am. And I do not know which is the more harmful, which the better: yet I do fear you more, Love, who with your glances kill more quickly the later you appear.

(Madrigal, possibly for 'the beautiful and cruel lady', 1544–5)‡

76

Un uomo in una donna, anzi uno dio
per la sua bocca parla,
ond'io per ascoltarla
son fatto tal, che ma' più sarò mio.
I' credo ben, po' ch'io   5
a me da lei fu' tolto,
fuor di me stesso aver di me pietate;
sì sopra 'l van desio
mi sprona il suo bel volto,
ch'i' veggio morte in ogni altra beltate.   10
O donna che passate
per acqua e foco l'alme a' lieti giorni,
deh, fate c'a me stesso più non torni.

77

Se ben concetto ha la divina parte
il volto e gli atti d'alcun, po' di quello
doppio valor con breve e vil modello
dà vita a' sassi, e non è forza d'arte.
Né altrimenti in più rustiche carte,   5
anz'una pronta man prenda 'l pennello,
fra ' dotti ingegni il più accorto e bello
pruova e rivede, e suo storie comparte.
Simil di me model di poca istima
mie parto fu, per cosa alta e prefetta   10
da voi rinascer po', donna alta e degna.
Se 'l poco accresce, e 'l mie superchio lima
vostra mercé, qual penitenzia aspetta
mie fiero ardor, se mi gastiga e 'nsegna?

78

Com'esser, donna, può quel c'alcun vede
per lunga sperïenza, che più dura
l'immagin viva in pietra alpestra e dura
che 'l suo fattor, che gli anni in cener riede?
La causa a l'effetto inclina e cede,   5

76

A man in a woman,* indeed a god speaks through her mouth, and so in listening to her I have become such that I shall never again be mine. I firmly believe, now that I have been taken from myself by her, that from outside myself I shall have pity on myself; so far above vain desire does her beautiful face spur me that I see death in every other beauty. O lady who passes souls through water and fire to happy days, bring this about, I beg you: that I may never again return to my own self.

(Madrigal, for Vittoria Colonna, 1544/5–6)

77

If a man's divine part has well conceived someone's face and gestures, it then through that double power, using a slight and lowly model, gives life to stones – and this is not the result of mere craftsmanship.

It operates no differently with regard to the roughest designs: before a ready hand may lift the brush, the divine part tries out and reworks the most interesting and beautiful of its fine ideas, then arranges its figures into a pattern.

So, too, with me: from birth I was made a model of little value, that I might then through you, noble and virtuous lady, be reborn as something noble and perfect.

If your kindness is to make the little I have increase, and file away my excess, what penitence awaits my fierce ardour, if it is to chastise and teach me?

(Sonnet, for Vittoria Colonna, 1544/5–6, revised 1546–50)

78

How can it be, lady, that, as long experience clearly shows, the living image in hard, alpine stone lasts longer than its maker, whom the years reduce again to dust?

The cause bows and yields to the effect, and so nature is conquered by art. This I know, who prove it in beautiful sculpture,

onde dall'arte è vinta la natura.
I' 'l so, che 'l pruovo in la bella scultura,
c'all'opra il tempo e morte non tien fede.
   Dunche, posso ambo noi dar lunga vita
in qual sie modo, o di colore o sasso,   10
di noi sembrando l'uno e l'altro volto;
   sì che mill'anni dopo la partita,
quante voi bella fusti e quant'io lasso
si veggia, e com'amarvi i' non fu' stolto.

79

   Negli anni molti e nelle molte pruove,
cercando, il saggio al buon concetto arriva
d'un'immagine viva,
vicino a morte, in pietra alpestra e dura;
c'all'alte cose nuove   5
tardi si viene, e poco poi si dura.
Similmente natura,
di tempo in tempo, d'uno in altro volto,
s'al sommo, errando, di belleza è giunta
nel tuo divino, è vecchia, e de' perire: 10
onde la tema, molto
con la beltà congiunta,
di stranio cibo pasce il gran desire;
né so pensar né dire
qual nuoca o giovi più, visto 'l tuo 'spetto,   15
o 'l fin dell'universo o 'l gran diletto.

80⁻

   S'egli è che 'n dura pietra alcun somigli
talor l'immagin d'ogni altri a se stesso,
squalido e smorto spesso
il fo, com'i' son fatto da costei.
E par ch'esempro pigli   5
ognor da me, ch'i' penso di far lei.
Ben la pietra potrei,
per l'aspra suo durezza,

that confronted with a work of art time and death fail in their task.

So I can give us both long life in either medium, whether in paint or stone, making a likeness of each of our faces;

so that a thousand years after we are gone people will be able to see how beautiful you were and how wretched I, and how in loving you I was not foolish.

(Sonnet, probably for Vittoria Colonna, *c.* 1545)‡

79

After many years and after many attempts, the wise artist succeeds in realizing a fine idea in a living image of hard, alpine stone only when he is near to death: for he comes late to fashioning what is noble and original, and he remains there for but a short time. So too with nature: if it has attained the height of beauty in your divine face only through trial and error, going from one period to the next, from one face to another, it is old and must soon perish. And so fear, closely linked to beauty, feeds my great desire with strange food; and I can neither know nor say whether, at the sight of your beautiful face, I am more harmed by the prospect of the end of the universe or helped by my great delight.

(Madrigal, possibly for Vittoria Colonna, *c.* 1542-5)‡

80

Since it is the case that, working in hard stone, the artist sometimes makes the image of everyone else resemble himself, I often make that woman's bleak and drear, as I am made by her. It seems that I always take myself as model when I set myself to fashion her. I could say that in its harsh hardness the very stone in which I model her resembles her; whatever about that, I simply am not able, while she destroys and despises me, to sculpt anything other than my afflicted features. But since art records beauty down

in ch'io l'esempro, dir c'a lei s'assembra;
del resto non saprei,   10
mentre mi strugge e sprezza,
altro sculpir che le mie afflitte membra.
Ma se l'arte rimembra
agli anni la beltà per durare ella,
farà me lieto, ond'io le' farò bella.   15

81

Se 'l duol fa pur, com'alcun dice, bello,
privo piangendo d'un bel volto umano,
l'essere infermo è sano,
fa vita e grazia la disgrazia mia:
ché 'l dolce amaro è quello   5
che, contr'a l'alma, il van pensier desia.
Né può fortuna ria
contr'a chi basso vola,
girando, trïonfar d'alta ruina;
ché mie benigna e pia   10
povertà nuda e sola,
m'è nuova ferza e dolce disciplina:
c'a l'alma pellegrina
è più salute, o per guerra o per gioco,
saper perdere assai che vincer poco.   15

82

– Se 'l volto di ch'i' parlo, di costei,
no' m'avessi negati gli occhi suoi,
Amor, di me qual poi
pruova faresti di più ardente foco,
s'a non veder me' lei   5
co' suo begli occhi tu m'ardi e non poco?
– La men parte del gioco
ha chi nulla ne perde,
se nel gioir vaneggia ogni desire:
nel sazio non ha loco   10
la speme e non rinverde

the ages, if she wishes to endure she will make me happy, so that I may make her beautiful.

(Madrigal, possibly for 'the beautiful and cruel lady', c. 1545)‡

81

If, as some say, suffering even makes a person beautiful, then since I am deprived of the sight of a beautiful human face, my being ill is healthy, my ungracious fate brings life and grace: for that sweetness is bitter which vain thought desires, contrary to the soul's good. Nor can evil fortune, turning its wheel, enjoy the triumph of casting down to ruin from a great height someone who flies low; for my naked and lonely poverty is yet kind and merciful, being a fresh whip and a sweet discipline: because to the pilgrim soul there is greater benefit, whether in war or in play, in knowing how to lose much than how to gain little.

(Madrigal, c. 1545)

82

'If the face of which I am speaking, her face, had not denied to me its eyes, Love, what further trial would you have set for me in a more fiercely burning fire, since even without my seeing more of her you burn me, and not a little, with her beautiful eyes?'

'He gains least from playing who in doing so loses nothing, for when joy is attained all desire disappears: in complete fulfilment there is no room for hope, which cannot flower again in the sweetness that banishes all suffering.'

'But in her case I wish to say: if she were to grant in great abundance what I aspire to, this reward from you would not quieten my high desire.'

(Madrigal, c. 1545–7)

nel dolce che preschive ogni martire –
– Anzi di lei vo' dire:
s'a quel c'aspiro suo gran copia cede,
l'alto desir non quieta tuo mercede.   15

83

Caro m'è 'l sonno, e più l'esser di sasso,
mentre che 'l danno e la vergogna dura;
non veder, non sentir m'è gran ventura;
però non mi destar, deh, parla basso.

84

Dal ciel discese, e col mortal suo, poi
che visto ebbe l'inferno giusto e 'l pio,
ritornò vivo a contemplare Dio,
per dar di tutto il vero lume a noi.

Lucente stella, che co' raggi suoi   5
fe' chiaro a torto el nido ove nacqui'io,
né sare' l' premio tutto 'l mondo rio;
tu sol, che la creasti, esser quel puoi.

Di Dante dico, che mal conosciute
fur l'opre suo da quel popolo ingrato   10
che solo a' iusti manca di salute.

Fuss'io pur lui! c'a tal fortuna nato,
per l'aspro esilio suo, co' la virtute,
dare' del mondo il più felice stato.

85

Quante dirne si de' non si può dire,
chè troppo agli orbi il suo splendor s'accese;
biasmar si può più 'l popol che l'offese,
c'al suo men pregio ogni maggior salire.

Questo discese a' merti del fallire   5
per l'util nostro, e poi a Dio ascese;
e le porte, che 'l ciel non gli contese,
la patria chiuse al suo giusto desire.

83*

Dear to me is sleep, dearer still being made of stone, while harm and shame last; not to see, not to hear, to me is a great boon; so do not waken me, ah, speak but softly.

(Quatrain, *c*. 1545–6)‡

84*

He came down from heaven,* and in his mortal body, after seeing both the just and the merciful hell,* returned alive to contemplate God, that he might give to us true light regarding all that he had seen.

A shining star, who with his rays made undeservedly famous the nest where I was born: for him the whole wicked world would not be adequate reward; you alone, who created him, can be such.

I speak of Dante, whose works were ill recognized by that ungrateful people which fails to bestow favour only on the just.

O that I were he! for were I born to such a destiny, I should exchange for his harsh exile, together with his virtue, the happiest state in all the world.

(Sonnet, *c*. 1545–6)‡

85*

All that should be said of him cannot be said, for too brightly did his splendour burn for our blind eyes; we can more easily reprove the people that wronged him than we can rise, even the greatest among us, to speak of his least merit.

For our good this man descended to where transgression has its just deserts, and then ascended to God; but the gates which heaven did not hold barred against him his native land closed to his just desire.

Ingrata, dico, e della suo fortuna
a suo danno nutrice; ond'è ben segno   10
c'a' più perfetti abonda di più guai.
    Fra mille altre ragion sol ha quest'una:
se par non ebbe il suo exilio indegno,
simil uom né maggior non nacque mai.

86

Nel dolce d'una immensa cortesia,
dell'onor, della vita alcuna offesa
s'asconde e cela spesso, e tanto pesa
che fa men cara la salute mia.
    Chi gli omer' altru' 'mpenna e po' tra via   5
a lungo andar la rete occulta ha tesa,
l'ardente carità d'amore accesa
là più l'ammorza ov'arder più desia.
    Però, Luigi mio, tenete chiara
la prima grazia, ond'io la vita porto,   10
che non si turbi per tempesta o vento.
    L'isdegno ogni mercé vincere impara,
e s'i' son ben del vero amico accorto,
mille piacer non vaglion un tormento.

87

Donn', a me vecchio e grave,
ov'io torno e rientro
e come a peso il centro,
che fuor di quel riposo alcun non have,
il ciel porge le chiave.   5
Amor le volge e gira
e apre a' iusti il petto di costei;
le voglie inique e prave
mi vieta, e là mi tira,
già stanco e vil, fra ' rari e semidei.   10
Grazie vengon da lei
strane e dolce e d'un certo valore,
che per sé vive chiunche per le' muore.

Ungrateful I declare that land, and nourisher of its destiny to its own harm; of which a clear sign is that it lavishes most troubles on those who are most perfect.

Among a thousand proofs that might be given let this alone suffice: just as no exile was ever less deserved than his, so no one of like worth or greater was ever born.

(Sonnet, *c.* 1545–6)‡

86*

Within the sweetness of an immense kindness there often lurks concealed some offence to one's honour and one's life; and this so weighs on me that it makes my good health less precious.

Anyone who gives wings to another's shoulders, and then along the way gradually spreads out a hidden net, extinguishes completely the ardent charity enkindled by love precisely where it most desires to burn.

So, my Luigi, keep shining clear that first graciousness, to which I owe my life, that it may not be troubled by storm or wind.

Offence manages to outweigh all kindness shown, and if I do indeed understand true friendship, then a thousand pleasures count less than a single torment.

(Sonnet for Luigi del Riccio, 1545–6)

87

Heaven offers to me, heavy with years, the keys of the lady to whom I turn and go back, as a weight does to the centre because nowhere else can it find repose. Love fits and turns them, and opens the heart of that lady to those who are just; she forbids me to have evil and depraved desires, and draws me up, tired and worthless though I am, among the godlike few. From her come graces strange and sweet and of such power that whoever dies for her lives for himself.

(Madrigal, possibly for Vittoria Colonna, possibly 1546)‡

88

Perché sì tardi e perché non piú spesso
con ferma fede quell'interno ardore
che mi lieva di terra e porta 'l core
dove per suo virtú non gli è concesso?
    Forse c'ogn' intervallo n'è promesso   5
da l'uno a l'altro tuo messo d'amore,
perc'ogni raro ha più forz'e valore
quant'è più desïato e meno appresso.
    La notte è l'intervallo, e 'l dì la luce:
l'una m'agghiaccia 'l cor, l'altro l'infiamma   10
d'amor, di fede e d'un celeste foco.

89

Quantunche sie che la beltà divina
qui manifesti il tuo bel volto umano,
donna, il piacer lontano
m'è corto sì, che del tuo non mi parto,
c'a l'alma pellegrina   5
gli è duro ogni altro sentiero erto o arto.
Ond' il tempo comparto:
per gli occhi il giorno e per la notte il core,
senza intervallo alcun c'al cielo aspiri.
Sì 'l destinato parto   10
mi ferm'al tuo splendore,
c'alzar non lassa i mie ardenti desiri,
s'altro non è che tiri
la mente al ciel per grazia o per mercede:
tardi ama il cor quel che l'occhio non vede.   15

90

Ben può talor col mie 'rdente desio
salir la speme e non esser fallace,
ché s'ogni nostro affetto al ciel dispiace,
a che fin fatto arebbe il mondo Iddio?
    Qual più giusta cagion dell'amart'io   5
è, che dar gloria a quella eterna pace
onde pende il divin che di te piace,

88

Why does it come so slowly and why not more often, that inner ardour full of firm faith, which lifts me from earth and bears my heart to where by its own power it is not permitted to go?

Perhaps every interval between one message of your love and the next is allotted us because everything rare has greater strength and value the more it is desired and the less near.

The interval is night, the light is day: one freezes my heart, the other inflames it with love, with faith and with a heavenly fire.

(Partial sonnet, possibly for Vittoria Colonna, possibly 1546)

89

Although it is true that your beautiful human face shows forth the divine beauty here, lady, my delight in that distant beauty is for me so fleeting that I cannot part from my delight in you, for to my pilgrim soul every other path, being steep and narrow, is too difficult. So I divide my time thus: my day is given to your eyes, by night my heart is with you, leaving no interval at all in which I may aspire to heaven. The destiny accorded me at birth so binds me to your splendour* that it does not allow me to raise my burning desires, if there be nothing else to draw my mind to heaven by grace or mercy: the heart is slow to love what the eye does not see.

(Madrigal, possibly for Vittoria Colonna, possibly 1546)‡

90

Hope can indeed at times ascend on high with my burning desire* and not prove false, for if all our emotions were displeasing to heaven, to what end would God have made the world?

What juster reason for my loving you can there be, than to give glory to that eternal peace from which derives the divine element in you that brings pleasure, and that makes every noble heart pure and devout?

e c'ogni cor gentil fa casto e pio?

    Fallace speme ha sol l'amor che muore
con la beltà c'ogni momento scema,   10
ond'è suggetta al variar d'un bel viso.

    Dolce è ben quella in un pudico core,
che per cangiar di scorza o d'ora strema
non manca, e qui caparra il paradiso.

91

    Non è sempre di colpa aspra e mortale
d'una immensa bellezza un fero ardore,
se poi sì lascia liquefatto il core,
che 'n breve il penetri un divino strale.

    Amore isveglia e desta e 'mpenna l'ale,   5
né l'alto vol preschive al van furore;
qual primo grado c'al suo creatore,
di quel non sazia, l'alma ascende e sale.

    L'amor di quel ch'i' parlo in alto aspira;
donna è dissimil troppo; e mal conviensi   10
arder di quella al cor saggio e verile.

    L'un tira al cielo, e l'altro in terra tira;
nell'alma l'un, l'altr'abita ne' sensi,
e l'arco tira a cose basse e vile.

92

    I' sto rinchiuso come la midolla
da la sua scorza, qua pover e solo,
come spirto legato in un'ampolla:

    e la mia scura tomba è picciol volo,
dov'è Aragn'e mill'opre e lavoranti,   5
e fan di lor filando fusaiuolo.

    D'intorn'a l'uscio ho mete di giganti,
ché chi mangi'uva o ha presa medicina
non vanno altrove a cacar tutti quanti.

    I' ho 'mparato a conoscer l'orina   10
e la cannella ond'esce, per quei fessi

False hope is harboured only by that love which dies with the beauty that is worn away by each passing minute, and so is subject to the variation wrought in a beautiful face.

Sweet indeed is the hope found in a chaste heart: it does not fail because of changes caused in the husk or brought by the final hour, and is here below a pledge of paradise.

(Sonnet, possibly for Tommaso Cavalieri, *c.* 1546)‡

91

To burn fiercely for an immense beauty is not always a harsh and deadly fault, if it so softens the heart that a divine arrow may then easily pierce it.

Love arouses and awakens us, and gives us feathered wings; it does not prevent vain passion from becoming a flight on high: this serves as a first step towards the creator for the soul, which, not satisfied with it, rises and ascends to him.

The love of which I am speaking aspires to the heights; it is too unlike a woman,* and to burn for one ill becomes a wise and manly heart.

The former shoots towards heaven, the latter shoots on earth; one dwells in the soul, the other in the senses, and looses the bow at low and worthless things.

(Sonnet, probably for Tommaso Cavalieri, 1546–7)

92*

I am shut in like a marrow by its skin, poor and alone here, like a genie trapped in a bottle,

and it would take little time to fly round my dark tomb,* where Arachne* and a thousand of her works and workers are, who as they spin make bobbins of themselves.

Around my doorway I have giant dung-heaps, for those who have eaten grapes or taken a laxative go nowhere else to dump the lot.

I have learned to become well acquainted with urine and the spout from which it comes, because of those cracks which before daybreak announce the morning to me.

che 'nanzi dì mi chiamon la mattina.

Gatti, carogne, canterelli o cessi,
chi n'ha per masserizi' o men vïaggio
non vien a vicitarmi mai senz'essi.   15

L'anima mia dal corpo ha tal vantaggio,
che se stasat' allentasse l'odore,
seco non la terre' 'l pan e 'l formaggio.

La toss' e 'l freddo il tien sol che non more;
se la non esce per l'uscio di sotto,   20
per bocca il fiato a pen' uscir può fore.

Dilombato, crepato, infranto e rotto
son già per le fatiche, e l'osteria
è morte, dov'io viv' e mangio a scotto.

La mia allegrezz' è la maninconia,   25
e 'l mio riposo son questi disagi:
che chi cerca il malanno, Dio gliel dia.

Chi mi vedess' a la festa de' Magi
sarebbe buono; e più, se la mia casa
vedessi qua fra sì ricchi palagi.   30

Fiamma d'amor nel cor non m'è rimasa;
se 'l maggior caccia sempre il minor duolo,
di penne l'alma ho ben tarpata e rasa.

Io tengo un calabron in un orciuolo,
in un sacco di cuoio ossa e capresti,   35
tre pilole di pece in un bocciuolo.

Gli occhi di biffa macinati e pesti,
i denti come tasti di stormento
c'al moto lor la voce suoni e resti.

La faccia mia ha forma di spavento;   40
i panni da cacciar, senz'altro telo,
dal seme senza pioggia i corbi al vento.

Mi cova in un orecchio un ragnatelo,
ne l'altro canta un grillo tutta notte;
né dormo e russ' al catarroso anelo.   45

Amor, le muse e le fiorite grotte,
mie scombiccheri, a' cemboli, a' cartocci,
agli osti, a' cessi, a' chiassi son condotte.

Che giova voler far tanti bambocci,
se m'han condotto al fin, come colui   50

Cats' corpses, turds, chamberpots or their contents, no one ever comes to visit me without leaving these, as offerings for the house or to save themselves a further journey.

My soul is so at ease in my body that if this were unstopped and let out its smell, I should not be able to keep my soul in it, even if I offered a good meal.

Only my coughs and colds prevent my body from dying; if my soul cannot get out the lower exit, my breath itself* can scarcely get out through my mouth.

I am by now worn out, ruptured,* crushed and broken by my labours, and death is my tavern, where I eat and stay at a price.

I find my happiness in melancholy,* and my rest in these discomforts: so may whoever seeks misfortune be granted it by God.

Were anyone to see me at the feast of the Ugly Old Woman,* he would think I'd do very well for the part; and all the more if he saw my house set here among such rich palaces.

No flame of love is to be found now in my heart; since greater suffering casts out the lesser, my soul has been well and truly clipped and shorn of its wings.

I possess a hornet in a jug,* bones and sinews in a leather sack, and three pills of pitch* in a little bottle.

My eyes are a bluish colour, as if they had been ground and pounded; my teeth are like the keys of an instrument, for as they move my voice sounds out and ceases.

My face is fit to terrify; my clothes, without further weapons, would be enough to scatter to the winds crows feeding on seeds in a dry field.

A cobweb sits brooding in one ear, in the other a cricket sings all night; and I cannot sleep and snore for my catarrhal breathing.

My scribblings* about love, the muses, flowery grottoes have ended up on tambourines, or as waste-paper in inns, latrines and brothels.

What was the good of having set myself to make so many rag dolls,* if they have led me to such an end, like someone who crossed the sea only to drown in snot?

The esteemed art,* through which at one time I was held in such high regard, has brought me to this: I am poor, old, and a slave in others' power,

so that I shall be a human wreck, if death does not come soon.

(*Capitolo*, 1546–50)

che passò 'l mar e poi affogò ne' mocci?
    L'arte pregiata, ov'alcun tempo fui
di tant'opinïon, mi rec'a questo,
povero, vecchio e servo in forz' altrui,
    ch'i' son disfatto, s'i' non muoio presto.   55

93

    Deh fammiti vedere in ogni loco!
Se da mortal bellezza arder mi sento,
appresso al tuo mi sarà foco ispento,
e io nel tuo sarò, com'ero, in foco.
    Signor mie caro, i' te sol chiamo e 'nvoco   5
contr'a l'inutil mie cieco tormento:
tu sol puo' rinnovarmi fuora e drento
le voglie e 'l senno e 'l valor lento e poco.
    Tu desti al tempo, Amor, quest'alma diva
e 'n questa spoglia ancor fragil e stanca   10
l'incarcerasti, e con fiero destino.
    Che poss'io altro che così non viva?
Ogni ben senza te, Signor, mi manca;
il cangiar sorte è sol poter divino.

94

    Passa per gli occhi al core in un momento
qualunche obbietto di beltà lor sia,
e per sì larga e sì capace via
c'a mille non si chiude, non c'a cento,
    d'ogni età, d'ogni sesso; ond'io pavento,   5
carco d'affanni, e più di gelosia;
né fra sì vari volti so qual sia
c'anzi morte mi die 'ntero contento.
    S'un ardente desir mortal bellezza
ferma del tutto, non discese insieme   10
dal ciel con l'alma; è dunche umana voglia.
    Ma se pass'oltre, Amor, tuo nome sprezza,
c'altro die cerca; e di quel più non teme
c'a lato vien contr'a sì bassa spoglia.

93

Ah make me see you present everywhere! If I feel myself burning for mortal beauty, that will be for me like a spent fire compared to yours, and in yours I shall be on fire, as I was before.

My dear Lord, you alone do I call on and invoke against my blind, futile torment; you alone can renew inside and out my will, my mind and my sluggish, feeble strength.

You, Love, awakened into time this divine soul, and in this covering, now fragile and weary, you imprisoned it, allotting it a harsh destiny.

What else can I do that I may not live this way? Every good without you, Lord, will fail me: to change a person's state belongs to divine power alone.

(Sonnet, 1547)

94*

Any object that* appears beautiful to my eyes passes through them to my heart in an instant, and by a path so wide and spacious that it would not be blocked by a thousand such, never mind a hundred,

of every age and of each sex; this makes me fearful, weighed down by troubles as I am, and even more by envy; nor do I know any face among so many different ones that might before death bring me complete happiness.

If mortal beauty entirely arrests an ardent desire, such a desire did not descend from heaven along with the soul; it is, therefore, a human willing.

But if it passes beyond,* Love, it scorns your name, for it seeks another god; and it no longer fears the fact that you are at our side warring against such a miserable covering.

(Sonnet, late, possibly 1547–50)

95

Se con lo stile o coi colori avete
alla natura pareggiato l'arte,
anzi a quella scemato il pregio in parte,
che 'l bel di lei più bello a noi rendete,
    poi che con dotta man posto vi sete   5
a più degno lavoro, a vergar carte,
quel che vi manca, a lei di pregio in parte,
nel dar vita ad altrui, tutta togliete.
    Che se secolo alcuno omai contese
in far bell'opre, almen cedale, poi   10
che convien c'al prescritto fine arrive.
    Or le memorie altrui, già spente, accese
tornando, fate or che fien quelle e voi,
malgrado d'esse, etternalmente vive.

96

La forza d'un bel viso a che mi sprona?
C'altro non è c'al mondo mi diletti:
ascender vivo fra gli spirti eletti
per grazia tal, c'ogni altra par men buona.
    Se ben col fattor l'opra suo consuona,   5
che colpa vuol giustizia ch'io n'aspetti,
s'i' amo, anz'ardo, e per divin concetti
onoro e stimo ogni gentil persona?

97

Con tanta servitù, con tanto tedio
e con falsi concetti e gran periglio
dell'alma, a sculpir qui cose divine.

98

Giunto è già 'l corso della vita mia,
con tempestoso mar, per fragil barca,

95*

If with your stylus* and your colours you have made art equal to nature, and indeed in part surpassed its achievement by making more beautiful for us the beauty found in it,

now that you have set yourself with learned hand to a more noble task, to writing, you have completely gained, by giving life to others, what was lacking in you and was nature's sole advantage.

For if any century has ever vied with nature in making works of beauty, it has always had to concede this to it, that all must finally arrive at their prescribed end.

Yet by rekindling the memories of men which had once been extinguished, you now bring it about that they, and you, despite nature, are eternally alive.

(Sonnet, for Giorgio Vasari, 1550)

96*

To what am I spurred by the power of a beautiful face? Since there is nothing else in the world that brings me delight: to ascend, while still alive, among the blessed spirits by a grace so great that every other seems inferior.

If every work is truly similar to its maker, what blame would justice have me expect, if I love, indeed burn, and honour and esteem every noble person as being divinely conceived?

(Partial sonnet, late)

97

To sculpt divine things here can be done only with great slavery and great tedium, with false ideas and with grave danger to the soul.

(Unrhymed tercet, c. 1552)

98*

My life's journey has finally arrived, after a stormy sea, in a fragile boat, at the common port, through which all must pass to

al comun porto, ov'a render si varca
conto e ragion d'ogni opra trista e pia.
    Onde l'affettüosa fantasia   5
che l'arte mi fece idol e monarca
conosco or ben com'era d'error carca
e quel c'a mal suo grado ogn'uom desia.
    Gli amorosi pensier, già vani e lieti,
che fien or, s'a duo morte m'avvicino?   10
D'una so 'l certo, e l'altra mi minaccia.
    Né pinger né scolpir fie più che quieti
l'anima, volta a quell'amor divino
c'aperse, a prender noi, 'n croce le braccia.

99

Le favole del mondo m'hanno tolto
il tempo dato a contemplare Iddio,
né sol le grazie suo poste in oblio,
ma con lor, più che senza, a peccar volto.
    Quel c'altri saggio, me fa cieco e stolto   5
e tardi a riconoscer l'error mio;
manca la speme, e pur cresce il desio
che da te sia dal propio amor disciolto.
    Ammezzami la strada c'al ciel sale,
Signor mie caro, e a quel mezzo solo   10
salir m'è di bisogno la tuo 'ita.
    Mettimi in odio quante 'l mondo vale
e quante suo bellezze onoro e colo,
c'anzi morte caparri eterna vita.

100

Non è più bassa o vil cosa terrena
che quel che, senza te, mi sento e sono,
onde a l'alto desir chiede perdono
la debile mie propia e stanca lena.
    Deh, porgi, Signor mio, quella catena   5
che seco annoda ogni celeste dono:
la fede, dico, a che mi stringo e sprono;

render an account and explanation of their every act, evil and devout.

So I now fully recognize how my fond* imagination which made art for me an idol and a tyrant was laden with error, as is that which* all men desire to their own harm.

What will now become of my former thoughts of love, empty yet happy, if I am now approaching a double death?* Of one I am quite certain, and the other threatens me.

Neither painting nor sculpting can any longer quieten my soul, turned now to that divine love which on the cross, to embrace us, opened wide its arms.

(Sonnet, 1552–4)

99

The fables of this world have taken from me the time given for contemplating God; and not only have I disregarded God's graces, but, because of these, I have more fully turned to sin than had I lacked them.

What makes others wise makes me blind and foolish, and slow to recognize the error of my ways; hope fades, and yet my desire increases that by you I may be freed from selfish love.*

Halve for me the road that climbs to heaven, my dear Lord; and even to climb that half I have need of your help.

Make me hate* all that the world values, and all its beauties that I honour and revere, so that before death I may lay hold of life eternal.

(Sonnet, sent to Monsignor Ludovico Beccadelli* in March 1555)

100*

No earthly thing is more base and vile than I feel myself to be, and am, without you, and so my own weak and tired breath begs pardon of you, who are supremely to be desired.

Ah, hold out to me, my Lord, that chain which comes bound round with every heavenly gift: faith, I mean, to which I press and spur myself, but of which through my own fault I lack the grace whole and entire.

né, mie colpa, n'ho grazia intiera e piena.
    Tanto mi fie maggior, quante più raro
il don de' doni, e maggior fia se, senza,   10
pace e contento il mondo in sé non have.
    Po' che non fusti del tuo sangue avaro,
che sarà di tal don la tuo clemenza,
se 'l ciel non s'apre a noi con altra chiave?

101

    Scarco d'un'importuna e greve salma,
Signor mie caro, e dal mondo disciolto,
qual fragil legno a te stanco rivolto
da l'orribil procella in dolce calma.
    Le spine e ' chiodi e l'una e l'altra palma   5
col tuo benigno umil pietoso volto
prometton grazia di pentirsi molto,
e speme di salute a la trist'alma.
    Non mirin co' iustizia i tuo sant'occhi
il mie passato, e 'l gastigato orecchio;   10
non tenda a quello il tuo braccio severo.
    Tuo sangue sol mie colpe lavi e tocchi,
e più abondi, quant'i' son più vecchio,
di pronta aita e di perdono intero.

102

    Penso e ben so c'alcuna colpa preme,
occulta a me, lo spirto in gran martire;
privo dal senso e dal suo propio ardire
il cor di pace, e 'l desir d'ogni speme.
    Ma chi è teco, Amor, che cosa teme   5
che grazia allenti inanzi al suo partire?

103

Carico d'anni e di peccati pieno

This gift of gifts will be to me all the greater for being so rare, and greater still since, without it, the world cannot in itself find peace and happiness.

Though you were not sparing of your blood, what good will be your mercy shown in such a gift, if heaven does not open itself to us with another key?*

(Sonnet, 1555)

101

Relieved of a troublesome and heavy burden, my dear Lord, and freed from the world, I turn wearily to you, like a fragile boat passing from a terrible storm to a pleasant calm.

The thorns and nails and both your palms, together with your kind, humble, merciful face, promise to the sinful soul the grace of deep repentance and the hope of salvation.

May your holy eyes and pure ears not respond with rigorous justice to my past life; may your severe arm not stretch out towards it.

May your blood alone cleanse and remove my sins; and may it more abound the older I am, with ready help and with complete forgiveness.

(Sonnet, late, possibly 1555 or after)

102

I think, indeed I know, that some guilt, hidden from me, oppresses my soul to the point of great torment, while by the senses and by its own boldness my heart is deprived of peace and my desire of all hope.

But if someone is close to you, Love, what can he fear that may weaken grace before his passing?

(Partial sonnet, late, possibly 1555 or after)

103

Burdened by years and full of sins and with my evil habits rooted

e col trist'uso radicato e forte,
vicin mi veggio a l'una e l'altra morte,
e parte 'l cor nutrisco di veleno.
　　Né propie forze ho, c'al bisogno sièno   5
per cangiar vita, amor, costume o sorte,
senza le tuo divine e chiare scorte,
d'ogni fallace corso guida e freno.
　　Signor mie car, non basta che m'invogli
c'aspiri al ciel sol perché l'alma sia,   10
non come prima, di nulla, creata.
　　Anzi che del mortal la privi e spogli,
prego m'ammezzi l'alta e erta via,
e fie più chiara e certa la tornata.

104

　　Mentre m'attrista e duol, parte m'è caro
ciascun pensier c'a memoria mi riede
il tempo andato, e che ragion mi chiede
de' giorni persi, onde non è riparo.
　　Caro m'è sol, perc'anzi morte imparo   5
quant'ogni uman diletto ha corta fede;
tristo m'è, c'a trovar grazi' e mercede
negli ultim'anni a molte colpe è raro.
　　Ché ben c'alle promesse tua s'attenda,
sperar forse, Signore, è troppo ardire   10
c'ogni superchio indugio amor perdoni.
　　Ma pur par nel tuo sangue si comprenda,
se per noi par non ebbe il tuo martire,
senza misura sien tuo cari doni.

105

　　Di morte certo, ma non già dell'ora,
la vita è breve e poco me n'avanza;
diletta al senso, è non però la stanza
a l'alma, che mi prega pur ch'i' mora.
　　Il mondo è cieco e 'l tristo esempro ancora   5
vince e sommerge ogni prefetta usanza;
spent'è la luce e seco ogni baldanza,

and strong, I see myself close to both deaths,* and still I nourish my heart with poison.

And I do not have powers of my own sufficient to change my life, love, conduct or condition, without your clear, divine help, which is guide and restraint for every treacherous journey.

My dear Lord, it is not enough for you simply to implant in me the will through which one aspires to heaven for my soul to be recreated, and not simply, as it was before, created from nothing.

Before you deprive and strip it of what is mortal, I beg you to halve for me the high, steep road, so that my return may be more clear and sure.

(Sonnet, late, possibly 1555 or after)

104

While I am saddened and pained by each one of them, those thoughts are yet dear to me that call to mind the time gone by and require me to give account of the lost days, which cannot be made up.

Dear to me only because I learn before death how short-lived is the promise given by every human pleasure; sad for me, because it is rare to find grace and mercy for many sins in one's final years.

For though one does rely on your promises, it is perhaps daring too much to hope, Lord, that love may pardon all excessive delay.

But still it seems that in your blood we are given to understand that, as for us your torment had no equal, so too your dear gifts may be without limit.

(Sonnet, late, possibly after 1555)

105

Certain of death, but not yet of its hour, I know that life is short and little of it left to me; though to remain here is delightful for the senses, it is not so for the soul, which indeed begs me to die.

The world is blind, and evil example still conquers and overwhelms even the noblest conduct; the light* has been extinguished, and with it all valour; falsehood triumphs and truth does not rise clear.

trionfa il falso e 'l ver non surge fora.
    Deh, quando fie, Signor, quel che s'aspetta
per chi ti crede? c'ogni troppo indugio   10
tronco la speme e l'alma fa mortale.
    Che val che tanto lume altrui prometta,
s'anzi vien morte, e senza alcun refugio
ferma per sempre in che stato altri assale?

106

    S'avvien che spesso il gran desir prometta
a' mie tant'anni di molt'anni ancora,
non fa che morte non s'appressi ognora,
e là dove men duol manco's affretta.
    A che più vita per gioir s'aspetta,   5
se sol nella miseria Iddio s'adora?
Lieta fortuna, e con lunga dimora,
tanto più nuoce quante più diletta.
    E se talor, tuo grazia, il cor m'assale,
Signor mie caro, quell'ardente zelo   10
che l'anima conforta e rassicura,
    da che 'l propio valor nulla mi vale,
subito allor sarie da girne al cielo:
ché con più tempo il buon voler men dura.

107

    Non fur men lieti che turbati e tristi
che tu patissi, e non già lor, la morte,
gli spirti eletti, onde le chiuse porte
del ciel, di terra a l'uom col sangue apristi.
    Lieti, poiché, creato, il redemisti   5
dal primo error di suo misera sorte;
tristi, a sentir c'a la pena aspra e forte,
servo de' servi in croce divenisti.
    Onde e chi fusti, il ciel ne diè tal segno
che scurò gli occhi suoi, la terra aperse,   10
tremorno i monti e torbide fur l'acque.

Ah, Lord, when will that happen which everyone who believes in you awaits? For all excessive delay cuts off hope and makes the soul mortal.*

What good is it that you promise us such great light, if in the meantime death overcomes us and forever binds us in that state in which it strikes us down?

(Sonnet, late, possibly after 1555)

106

If it often happens that strong desire promises my advanced years many years more, this does not mean that death does not draw closer every hour, or that it hastens more slowly to him who is less troubled by it.

Why does one look for longer life to enjoy oneself, if it is only in misery that God is adored?* Good fortune together with long life bring greater harm the more they bring delight.

And if at times through your grace, my dear Lord, that burning zeal assails my heart which comforts and reassures the soul,

since my own powers do not afford me any help at all, then would be the very moment to rise to heaven: for with more time good will in us lasts less.

(Sonnet, late, 1555 or after)

107

The blessed spirits were no less glad than troubled and sad that you, not they themselves, suffered death, by which with your blood you opened from on earth to man the closed gates of heaven.

Glad, because you redeemed man, created by you, from his wretched state caused by the first sin; sad, in knowing that it was through harsh and bitter pain that you became servant of the servants on the cross.

Whence you came and who you were, heaven showed us through these signs: it darkened its own eyes, and opened the earth, the mountains trembled and the waters were convulsed.

It took the great patriarchs from the realm of darkness, and

Tolse i gran Padri al tenebroso regno,
gli angeli brutti in più doglia sommerse;
godé sol l'uom, c'al battesmo rinacque.

108

Al zucchero, a la mula, a le candele,
aggiuntovi un fiascon di malvagia,
resta sì vinta ogni fortuna mia,
ch'i' rendo le bilance a san Michele.
Troppa bonaccia sgonfia sì le vele,   5
che senza vento in mar perde la via
la debile mie barca, e par che sia
una festuca in mar rozz'e crudele.
A rispetto a la grazia e al gran dono,
al cib', al poto e a l'andar sovente   10
c'a ogni mi' bisogno è caro e buono,
Signor mie car, ben vi sare' nïente
per merto a darvi tutto quel ch'i' sono:
ché 'l debito pagar non è presente.

109

Per croce e grazia e per diverse pene
son certo, monsignor, trovarci in cielo;
ma prima c'a l'estremo ultimo anelo,
goderci in terra mi parria pur bene.
Se l'aspra via coi monti e co 'l mar tiene   5
l'un da l'altro lontan, lo spirto e 'l zelo
non cura intoppi o di neve o di gelo,
né l'alia del pensier lacci o catene.
Ond'io con esso son sempre con voi,
e piango e parlo del mio morto Urbino,   10
che vivo or forse saria costà meco,
com'ebbi già in pensier. Sua morte poi
m'affretta e tira per altro cammino,
dove m'aspetta ad albergar con seco.

buried the vile angels in deeper suffering; only man rejoiced, for he was reborn through baptism.

(Sonnet, late)

108

The sugar, the mule, the candles, to which was added a flagon of malmsey: these so outweigh all my resources that I am handing back the scales to St Michael.

Too much calm weather has taken the wind from my sails so completely that my fragile boat lies lost on a windless sea, or seems like a wisp of straw on a rough and cruel sea.

Compared with your kindness and your great gifts – the food, the drink, the means of moving readily around, which is something very welcome and helpful for all my needs –

my dear lord, I should count as nothing in terms of merit, even were I to give you all that I am: for it is no present to repay a debt.

(Sonnet, possibly for Giorgio Vasari, late)

109*

Through the cross and grace and through our various sufferings, I am certain, monsignor, that we shall meet in heaven; but I am quite sure that it is right, before we finally breathe our last, to go on enjoying one another on earth.

If a harsh journey over mountain and sea keeps us far from each other, the spirit and ardent love care nothing for such obstacles as snow and ice, nor do the wings of thought know snares or chains.

So in thought I am always with you, and with you I weep as I speak of my dead Urbino,* who, were he still alive, would perhaps be over there with me now,

as I once had in mind. But instead his death hurries and draws me along another path, to where he is waiting for me to lodge with him.

(Sonnet, for Monsignor Ludovico Beccadelli, probably 1556)

Notes

1

There is no documentary evidence connected with this poem, or indeed with any other, that Michelangelo had a passionate sexual attraction to a woman. The evidence points overwhelmingly to Michelangelo's having been homosexual in orientation (though see poem 94 below). Poems such as the present one seem best regarded as exercises in a poetic tradition.

2

A self-mocking lament by Michelangelo on his troubles as he painted the ceiling of the Sistine Chapel (on which he worked from 1508–12).
14 Syrian bow: a semicircular bow, renowned for its effectiveness.
20 nor indeed a painter: Michelangelo always regarded himself principally as a sculptor.

3

A vigorous complaint against a patron by whom Michelangelo felt himself betrayed. Although it is impossible to determine with certainty the identity of the patron, details of the poem suggest Pope Julius II (1503–13).

4

In this vigorous lament Michelangelo is not concerned principally, as he was in poem 3, with his personal situation, but with the general condition of Rome (where the poem was written).
11 he who wears the mantle: the pope (*il gran manto* = the papal mantle).
11 can do what Medusa did in Mauritania: petrify through neglect or hostility.
14 another standard: a reference either to war or to money.

5

Not the least value of this mock love poem is that it reminds us that Michelangelo had a strong comic element in his character, and that he was capable of viewing the passions of love with irony. This suggests that many

of his love poems which make heavy use of conventional imagery ought not
to be taken with anything like total seriousness.

1 must: i.e., new wine.

6 theriac: a medicinal salve of a yellowish ('treacle') colour, thought to be
an antidote to poison.

14 a Syrian bow: see poem 2:14, and the note there.

9

A strikingly positive view of human love as the means of *entrée* to the divine,
a view shared by several poems of this period (e.g., 11–12); this view will
later animate many of Michelangelo's finest love poems, particularly those
dedicated to Tommaso Cavalieri.

8 my great desire: in Michelangelo's poetry (as in religious thought
generally) man's supreme desire is said to be for God, regarded as the
perfection of beauty, goodness, etc.

10 the eternal beauty: God, or the perfect idea of beauty in God's mind.

10

The addressee of this poem is not specified; it seems to be personified Love,
conceived as a quasi creative intermediary between the divine and the
human.

11

9–11 Love is a concept born of beauty . . .: an important, if dense and
elliptic, expression of Michelangelo's positive view of love.

13

One of the clearest expressions of Michelangelo's delight in human beauty
in its fulness, physical and spiritual. He is particularly deeply indebted here
to Petrarch.

14

2 the beauty that I long for: i.e., perfect, unlimited beauty, to be
identified with God.

10 a better place: the mind or soul.

12–13 There it becomes divine . . .: essential to the logic of these lines is
the idea that the soul is by its very nature immortal, to which quality the
other three (being divine, virtuous and beautiful) are inextricably linked.

15

Written after the death either of an intimate friend or of Michelangelo's brother Buonarroto (d. 1528), the only one of his siblings to whom he appears to have been close.

6 and all the more itself: in strict Christian terms an unorthodox sentiment, since God (here imaged as 'that divine hammer') was traditionally held to be totally immutable, unchanged even by his creative and providential activity.

21

10 what you most love in yourself: the soul or spiritual element.

23

12 if fire ... to the heavens: in contemporary physics the upward movement of fire was explained by the fire's seeking to return (like all beings) to its natural location, which in this case was thought to be a sphere above the air surrounding the earth.

24

8 from hell: according to Catholic doctrine, souls who die repentant but still marked by the effects of their former sins must have the latter purged before they may enter heaven and see God. In Michelangelo's time the realm in which this purification was achieved was often regarded as a section of hell.

25

10 may you atone for my sin: according to christian doctrine, serious sin rendered its agent unjust in the eyes of God, a state which could only be rectified by the application to the sinner of the perfect merits of Christ.

26

14 in my unworthy ... arms: the only direct expression of physical yearning for Cavalieri (or any male) in the final version of any of Michelangelo's poetry, apart from the curious conceits of poem 41; there may be indirect references at 37:3-4 and, though with less likelihood, at 43:14 (see the note there).

30

9 he who speaks for me: the unidentified bearer of this poetic letter from Michelangelo in Florence to Cavalieri in Rome.

13 pictures of the basest kind: we know that Michelangelo gave Cavalieri a number of drawings, almost certainly with the object of helping the young man to master the art of drawing. It seems likely that in using the strong adjective *turpissime* here Michelangelo was being heavily self-deprecatory, rather than pleading guilty to sexual impropriety in the pagan subjects of his drawings.

31

8 the intellect on God: God as infinite eludes adequate comprehension by the human mind.

35

This *capitolo* was composed in response to one of similar length by Francesco Berni (1497/8–1535), a burlesque poet. Berni's poem was sent to a common friend in Rome, the painter-cleric Sebastiano del Piombo (1485–1547), but was clearly intended for Michelangelo. Michelangelo responded in kind, with a poem purporting to be from del Piombo, although he himself is the fictitious bearer (lines 43–4).

4–6 the greatest Doctor . . .: Pope Clement VII, Giulio de' Medici; the periphrasis puns on *medico* (doctor).

7–9 He who . . . is served by you . . .: Cardinal Ippolito de' Medici, a cousin of the pope, termed 'the lesser Doctor' at line 11.

10–12 him who holds . . .: Cardinal Ippolito's secretary, the humanist writer Francesco Maria Molza.

19–21 The Meat . . .: Monsignor Pietro Carnesecchi, whose name lent itself to a double pun, on *carne* (meat) and *secco* (dry). The lines now have a bitter ring which was no part of the original intent: Carnesecchi was much later (in 1567) beheaded on charges of heresy and his body burned.

28–30 These will be harmed . . .: Michelangelo is parodying the notion that poetry, like all art, is immortal: Berni's comic poetry was often rough and plebeian in tone.

32–6 Votive offerings . . .: in his poem Berni had played on the common reference to Michelangelo as divine.

54 lose my cowl: del Piombo had become a religious in 1531, a condition of his taking up the post he had been offered at the papal court, Keeper of the Seal (*piombo*, lead).

36

13 spouse: an image often used in christian writings for the Church in general or for the individual soul.

39

13–14 I restore light . . . cure every poison: Michelangelo's comparison of himself to Christ is striking.

41

The 'lowly worm' so admired and envied in this poem is the silkworm.

42

9–11: the logic appears to be that the art of creating beauty surpasses nature because it comes from heaven; its heavenly origin enables it to outdo nature, even though the latter does perform well, and creates its own limited beauty.

43

14 armed cavalier: clearly a pun on Cavalieri's name. Some would see this as a sexual pun, a view at best marginally strengthened by *nudo* in line 13, since the latter can be used very generically in Italian, and is so understood in the translation.

46

4 him who . . . : God.
5 equal to himself: this most unusual description presumably refers to the soul's being equal to God only in being immortal.
8 beauty's universal form: in Neoplatonic philosophy, beauty is conceived as existing without limitation (perfectly, 'universally') in God.

47

13 veil: a common Petrarchan and Neoplatonic image for the human body; the soul, by contrast, is immortal.

49

There seems no reason to doubt the veracity of the account appended to this poem by Michelangelo's great-nephew: 'Bernardo [Buontalenti] said that Michelangelo halfway up his stairwell had drawn in black and white the figure of death as a skeleton bearing a rough coffin on its shoulder, on which [these lines] were written.'

50

Perhaps the first poem to have been inspired by Vittoria Colonna (1490–1547). A member of one of Rome's most illustrious noble families,

she married the Marchese di Pescara in 1509. This brave soldier but
faithless husband died in the service of the emperor in 1525, leaving her
childless. Colonna was a woman of great culture and deep religious
devotion, and a considerable poetess. Michelangelo was introduced to her
around 1536; she became for him a trusted friend who attracted him by her
moral rectitude and cultured religious devotion. He certainly dedicated a
number of poems to her, perhaps as many as forty.

9 the eye that does not see: i.e., the physical eye, which does not see
divine things.

51

14 the first love: i.e., the love of the first good, God.

52

Almost forty of Michelangelo's poems have traditionally been assigned a
dedication to a woman described, from the content of the poems, as 'la
donna bella e crudele'; for the sake of information, those dedications are
recorded in this translation. However, there is no documentary evidence of
his having been passionately in love with any woman in the way described
in these poems: see note to poem 1. Few of these poems are of significant
quality.

59

9–10 can so remove from my outer being: only through the influence
of Colonna will Michelangelo's outer being, physical and sensual, dominate
him less, and thus allow the good works within to emerge.

60

11 such narrow spaces: the eyes.

66

1 Sometimes . . . my left: the right foot was symbolic of virtue, the left of
vice.

68

3 both the arts: sculpting and painting.

71

This is taken from a series of fifty poems, all but two of them quatrains, sent
to Michelangelo's friend and financial agent, Luigi del Riccio, in the course

of the year following the death of his beloved nephew Cecchino [Francesco] Bracci in January 1544. Michelangelo's poems are in part a way of making up to del Riccio for his refusal fully to comply with his friend's request that he sculpt Cecchino's tomb: this was indeed designed by Michelangelo, but executed by his untalented if loyal assistant Urbino.

76

1 A man in a woman: the words read strangely, not to say offensively, today, although they were clearly intended as a compliment.

83

The Florentine academician Giovanni di Carlo Strozzi penned a laudatory if rather flat quatrain in praise of Michelangelo's statue of Night located in the Medici funerary chapel in Florence; Michelangelo found it unwelcome, presumably irritated that such praise should come from one who was closely, if perhaps innocently, associated with the repressive regime of Duke Cosimo I there.

84

The first of two poems (see also 85) on Dante. Michelangelo was regarded in his time as an expert on his Florentine predecessor.
1 He came down from heaven: indirectly, perhaps Michelangelo's highest praise of Dante, since the words echo clearly a phrase from the Latin creed expressing belief in Christ's divine origin: *descendit de caelis.*
2 the just and the merciful hell: respectively hell proper, where unrepentant sinners are eternally punished, and that part of hell where sinners who repented before death are purged of the effects of sin and prepare for heaven; see also the note to 24:8. Lines 2–3 refer to the three parts of Dante's journey in *The Divine Comedy*, through Hell and Purgatory to Heaven.

85

See introductory note to poem 84.

86

This and the following poem show Michelangelo at his least appealing as a person: so sensitive to real or presumed slight from an old and devoted friend, Luigi del Riccio, that he is prepared to regret the very health which he owes to del Riccio's generous care in offering him the hospitality of his own apartments in the Palazzo Strozzi when he was seriously ill.

89

11 splendour: the manifestation in finite beauty of the infinite God.

90

1 my burning desire: this phrase seems clearly to refer to love of a human being.

91

10 it is too unlike a woman: love for women was unflatteringly compared to love for men in the Neoplatonist tradition.

92

A highly ironic, yet moving, autobiographical sketch. With poem 35, this is one of Michelangelo's only two successful long poems; it is notable that both poems treat their subjects humorously and are written in the same poetic genre. Lines 1–6 introduce the two main themes: Michelangelo's body, and his physical surroundings. Lines 7–15 concentrate on the latter, lines 16–45 on the former. It is only in the final lines, 46–55, where Michelangelo turns to consider his cultural achievements, that bitterness overwhelms the comic tone.

4 my dark tomb: Michelangelo's house. It seems in fact to have been of modest size, rather than genuinely cramped as this and the following lines would suggest.

5 Arachne . . .: an oblique reference to the cobwebs with which Michelangelo's house must have abounded.

21 my breath itself . . .: Michelangelo's soul, then, has even less chance of escaping by that route.

22 I am . . . ruptured . . .: it is possible that *crepato* refers to Michelangelo's hernia condition.

25 I find . . . in melancholy: one of Michelangelo's most open acknowledgements of his depressive nature.

28 the feast of the Ugly Old Woman: for the sake of English readers who may be unfamiliar with Italian customs, the translation here takes a liberty with the text, which speaks simply of 'the feast of the Magi': this feast is, of course, that of the Epiphany (*l'Epifania*), when the Magi were shown the Christ child (according to the account of *Matthew* 2:9–12). In Italy during the night of this feast (6 January) gifts were traditionally put out for children, unless they were thought not to deserve them, in which case they were left ashes and coal; both kinds of 'present' were supposedly left by an old woman who came down the chimney. The old woman took on the name of the feast in its popular form, *la Befana*; she became proverbial for an old hag, the point to which Michelangelo is alluding here.

34 a hornet in a jug: almost certainly a reference to tinnitus.

36 three pills of pitch . . .: perhaps kidney stones, from which Michelangelo suffered.

46–8 My scribblings . . .: an ironic reference to Michelangelo's love poetry.

49 rag dolls: in the light of lines 52–4, the reference here is presumably to Michelangelo's visual art in general, rather than simply to his sculpture.

52 The esteemed art: sculpture.

94

A remarkable testimony to Michelangelo's attraction to human beauty in both male and female; this should temper the undoubtedly just ascription to him of a homosexual orientation.

2 Any object that . . .: line 5 makes clear that by 'object' Michelangelo has in mind only human beings; this is a notable indication of what is apparent from his art and poetry as a whole, that his concern was almost exclusively with human beauty.

12 passes beyond: i.e., beyond merely mortal beauty.

95

The year 1550 saw the publication of what turned out to be an epoch-making work in art history, Vasari's *Le vite de' più eccellenti pittori scultori e architettori*; the author sent Michelangelo a copy, and in the present poem Michelangelo offers his compliments and thanks.

1 with your stylus: this instrument is undoubtedly meant to signify drawing, as 'colours' does painting.

96

This is the most significant expression in Michelangelo's later years of the passion for human beauty that had inspired him through most of his life, a passion that is, however, explicitly or implicitly rejected in much of his late, narrowly exclusivist christian poetry.

98

This is justly regarded as one of Michelangelo's finest poems, despite its heavily negative evaluation of his artistic endeavours.

5 fond: *affettüosa* indicates a harmful dominance of the emotions.

8 that which . . .: this line may refer generically to a tendency in all human beings to make some finite thing their supreme good instead of God (as Michelangelo had done with art), or it may be speaking specifically of love.

10 a double death: the temporal death of the body and the eternal death of the soul, both clearly referred to at line 11.

99

On Monsignor Beccadelli see note on poem 109.

8 selfish love: literally, 'own love'; it seems better to avoid the term 'self-love', since the Catholic tradition did not condemn love of self as such, but only an excess of such love, to the exclusion of God and one's neighbour. It may be, though, that Michelangelo is careless of orthodoxy at this point; certainly poems such as 100 indicate a perilously high degree of self-disgust.

12 Make me hate . . .: perhaps the strongest repudiation in Michelangelo's late poetry of the beauty in which he had earlier found such inspiration, human and divine.

100

This poem is the most direct expression of the importance Michelangelo attached to the virtue of faith, a central and contentious subject in Reformation debates.

14 another key: it is clear that Michelangelo is referring to faith, the subject of lines 1–11: faith is the key which corresponds in the subjective realm to that of the redemption effected by Christ's death in the objective realm.

103

3 both deaths: see note 98:10.

105

7 the light: of grace, presumably.

11 mortal: i.e., subject to death, contrary to the soul's intrinsic immortality.

106

6 if it is only in misery that God is adored: religiously, perhaps Michelangelo's single most pessimistic line.

109

A measured, though warm and moving, expression of Michelangelo's inability to accept an invitation to visit from his long-standing friend Monsignor Ludovico Beccadelli, a religiously liberal prelate who had in effect just been banished from Rome by the conservative administration of Pope Paul IV to the archbishopric of Ragusa in distant Dalmatia (see also poem 99). The quietly positive view of the world in the octave contrasts with the tone of most of the late poetry.

10 Urbino: Michelangelo's loyal assistant and servant for over a quarter of a century, who died unexpectedly in December 1555.